liverpool

regeneration of a city centre

Author: David Taylor

with Terry Davenport

Designed by BDP

Published by BDP.

Looking north towards the
Mersey Estuary – Liverpool
One in the Heart of the City.

contents

introduction
by terry davenport

i

It's very rare to lead an undertaking that transforms the fortunes of a great city. It's even more unusual for that city to be your home town and place of birth. Because of my personal familiarity it has been a great privilege for me to have led the Liverpool One masterplan team, on behalf of Grosvenor, from the first day of the project. This publication is the story of the masterplan's evolution and the subsequent design development process.

In the summer of 1999 when the Paradise Street Development Area (PSDA) competition was launched, Liverpool was undergoing its first significant regeneration programme for many years. To the south, in Speke, Liverpool Land was progressing major improvements to one of the city's main arrival routes and in the city centre BDP was planning the Ropewalks regeneration initiative. However, prior to these undertakings, the city had witnessed a difficult 20 to 30 year period when its reputation was sadly forged not by the status of its wonderful heritage but by strikes, unrest and political upheaval. However, all that was to change with the council's drive for regeneration, the selection of Grosvenor as the development partner and their subsequent contribution to the city's remarkable recovery.

The challenge for the project team was enormous; to effectively rebuild a 42 acre swathe of the city centre through a 2.4 million sq ft mixed use retail led scheme thus leapfrogging the city's position in the retail hierarchy from a lowly 17th national ranking to a top five position. At the same time, to develop the project in such a way that seamlessly linked the development to the existing grain and street pattern of the city's remarkable heritage. All this to be ultimately conceived, designed, approved, constructed and fitted out in an eight year period plus, of course, all the enormous infrastructure works required for such an initiative.

The public support for the project was evident from the outset. So many disappointments over so many past years meant that the public's appetite for change was tangible. Grosvenor's exemplary consultation process engaged with the community at every level. The overarching public mood was supportive, despite the recognised challenges and inevitable disruption that lay ahead.

By any standards the Liverpool One project has been a huge team effort, not least across BDP. Over 60 architects from BDP have worked on the project across four locations, plus the partnering with our French associates - Groupe 6 SA. Our role has included developing and monitoring the masterplan through the life of the project, producing concept designs for six buildings and progressing the executive delivery of nine buildings through to completion; in total almost half of the project. Many successful collaborations were formed, not least through BDP and Pelli Clarke Pelli on the development of the 'Pool and the Park'. The many technical challenges that faced the teams are not encompassed in this design led story but BDP's collaboration with Laing O'Rourke was key to delivering a large part of the western side of Liverpool One with Balfour Beatty also playing a significant role to the east. In addition, BDP's landscape and lighting colleagues led a similar process across virtually the entire public realm, on the masterplan, concept and executive delivery fronts.

Ten years since the launch of the initial brief, the City Council, Grosvenor and the team can look back with pride at the achievement and the undoubted impact that Liverpool One has had on the city, its visitors and proud inhabitants. However, more importantly in these uncharted times, the challenge to the industry is how to maintain the regeneration of our towns and cities under a quite different set of circumstances, circumstances which mean that for the UK at least the scale of Liverpool One's achievement will not be repeated for many years to come. Aspiration levels, partnering agreements, delivery mechanisms, planning and phasing strategies will undoubtedly be rescaled to address the next chapter of development. BDP, with half a century of experience and thought leadership, is well placed to respond to the new challenges ahead and we look forward to working in partnership with local authorities, developers, institutions and contractors to continue our success in the regeneration of cities, towns and public places.

Terry Davenport. BDP Director

a historical overview of liverpool

1

historic influences

Liverpool's history has been shaped primarily by its geography. For centuries, the city has capitalised on its natural position at the mouth of the Mersey - from the port activities which catapulted its economy into prosperity, right through to its latter-day regeneration at the water's edge.

Indeed, one of the major natural advantages Liverpool has is that it sits on the Mersey tidal estuary. The historic centre of Liverpool - the former site of the castle, where the crown courts are now located - was on a high point overlooking the estuary. Beneath it was a small creek. This was called, from the Old English, 'Lifrigor pool' or 'muddy creek' - the origin of the city's name - where small ships would take refuge from the huge tidal surge. And so it began.

Much of the city's history is well documented, but there are a few key early milestones that are worth repeating. The first record of Liverpool as a settlement was 800 years ago on its foundation as a borough in 1207, when it was established by King John as a place from which he could embark to Ireland on his military forays. Connections to the country have stayed strong ever since.

It remained a relatively small place until the mid-seventeenth and eighteenth century, up until which point, in the age of exploration and maritime expansion, Bristol had been the major western port of Britain. Liverpool, though, was a focus for Atlantic trade - the triangular run between Africa, America and back again, and was also fundamental to Britain's growing Empire. All of which meant that Liverpool started to establish itself very rapidly as a major seaport, expanding initially to the south.

This page: Top; Liverpool Castle, circa 15th century, by Edward Fox. (LRO).
Left; Map of Liverpool, c1650 [Thomas Kaye, 1829]. (LRO).

maritime beginnings

8 A key date in Liverpool's rapid upward economic movement came with the development of its Old Dock. In 1708, Liverpool's port authorities set up a committee to develop the port, and appointed Thomas Steers to advise on the building of a dock system. Steers was one of the first of England's major civil engineers, having designed a series of canals, but his first recommendation was to abandon the idea of a canal system, and put forward the proposal to convert the Pool into a commercial wet dock controlled by floodgates.

BDP architect director Ken Moth takes up the story: 'Historically, if ports are affected by tidal range, then a lot of the time they can't operate because all the ships simply get grounded on the mud. So on the site of this muddy creek Steers proposed to build an impounded area, a masonry basin with a gate - it was the world's first commercial wet dock.'

It was also a brave step on the part of the city fathers. 'The burghers of Liverpool basically had to mortgage the town to pay for this to be built', says Moth. 'It was a very bold stroke, but it paid dividends.'

The site of that old dock, the Liverpool Old Dock, sits within what is the Paradise Street Development, or Liverpool One, today - some of the remains of its old wall are still visible through a special viewing window set into the ground on site. The line of the old creek was where Hanover Street winds down to meet the Strand.

Subsequently, more docks were built, until by the eighteenth century, four wet docks were in operation. Warehousing was also built, and as a direct result the trade in the city grew exponentially, along with the rise of Empire and aided by the fact that Liverpool was an Atlantic-facing port.

But it was the involvement of the city in instigating these improvements, says Moth, which proved to be the major catalyst.

Midway through the nineteenth century a separate body was set up - the Mersey Docks and Harbour Board - which built some 13 miles of wet docks out into the river. The entire major dock infrastructure, starting with the Albert Dock, the Pier Head and all the docks north and south, are all built out into the river on timber piles and feature massive masonry walls. 'It was an absolutely stupendous piece of engineering, the like of which was not seen anywhere else in the nineteenth century', adds Moth. 'But it started off on the Paradise Street site.'

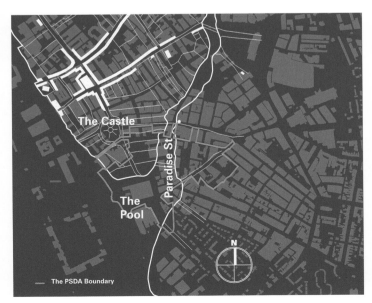

The Castle

Paradise St

The Pool

N

— The PSDA Boundary

Old Dock

N

— The PSDA Boundary

Opposite page: The
Emerging City. Figures taken
from the PSDA masterplan
illustrating the developing
street pattern and waterfront.
(BDP). **Left:** The Origin of
Liverpool. *(BDP).* **Right;**
Liverpool as a commercial
city, c1766. *(BDP).*

This page: Top; Ackerman's
view of Liverpool with Albert
Dock in the foreground,
c1847. *(LRO / LCC).*
Bottom; John Eyres' map
of Liverpool with the PSDA
project boundary overlaid,
c1765. *(LRO).*

Opposite page: Top; View from Salthouse Dock to the
Custom House, 1890. (LRO / LCC).
Bottom; Romantic view of the Liverpool Waterfront,
1865. (LRO / LCC).

This page: Top; View from Canning Half Tide Dock looking
towards Custom House, 1890. (Black & White Picture Place)
Right; Albert Dock crowded with schooners and other
vessels, 1924. (Black & White Picture Place).

This page: PSDA boundary outline superimposed over circa 17th & 18th century maps. This clearly shows the location of the old dock and the city's radiating street pattern. (Maps, LRO).

Opposite: City evolution. A series of snapshots illustrating the initial growth, decline and re-emergence of the main retail area.

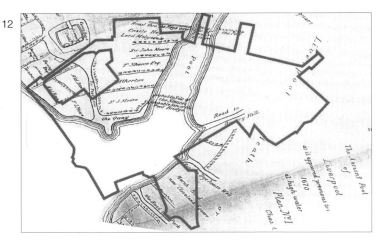
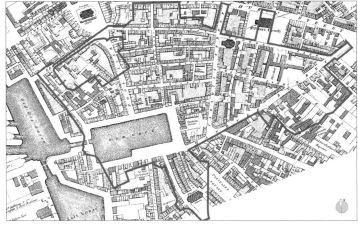

It is worth pausing here to reflect on the historical context, and look graphically at some of the retail precedents and Liverpool's urban grain; to turn the clock back a little. The medieval picture was essentially of a city laid out on six main streets - said to have been designed by King John himself - in an 'H' shape leading down to the river. Liverpool was one of the very few planned towns in the north-west, with this grid of six streets set out on a sandstone ridge alongside the tidal creek of the Mersey. A seventh street, Castle Street, probably came about following the creation of the castle in around 1235 to the south west of the centre. This street pattern remained largely unchanged from the late thirteenth to the late seventeenth century.

But it was in the period between 1680 and 1800 that the city was transformed from having a port that was dwarfed by London's bustling wharves and quays to become the leading provincial port in England. Largely this transition came about through the mercantile elite dominating and establishing a firm grip on urban government. Mercantile networks provided the commercial revolution, the city capitalising on growing sugar and tobacco trades with the West Indian and north American colonies.

Moving on, Horwood's map of 1803 shows a detailed layout of the Georgian port, showing the street layout of roughly rectangular blocks, the frequency of street varying between 30m to 150m, with the Old Dock occupying an area some 100 x 200 m to the south west. During the nineteenth century, the general trend was for rear garden courts to be gradually eroded by in-fill development, and for a substantial proportion of Georgian domestic plots to be amalgamated to make way for banks, theatres, office chambers and shops, but on a relatively small scale.

To the south east of the old castle site was the area where all the ropes and rigging were made to serve the maritime industry. 'Ropewalks' were long, external stretches of land where ropes were made, and that is still the name of the wider area today. This Liverpool district was laid out in the eighteenth century on a formal Georgian grid with merchants' houses and warehouses. This was the real Georgian heart of Liverpool.

These historical precedents and street patterns - the city's urban grain - have driven the layout of the Liverpool One site and enabled BDP's designers to look to stitch together the urban fabric and create a masterplan with distinctive urban 'quarters', but more of that later.

This part of Liverpool is very important historically, representing where the city and the port originated. It was certainly a successful format - by the early nineteenth century, some 40% of the world's trade was passing through Liverpool's docks, contributing to Liverpool's rise as a major city.

It was, in short, becoming a global destination - for trade, people, and culture.

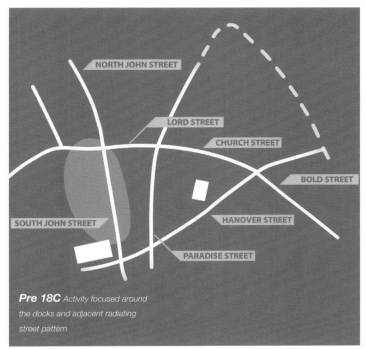

Pre 18C *Activity focused around the docks and adjacent radiating street pattern*

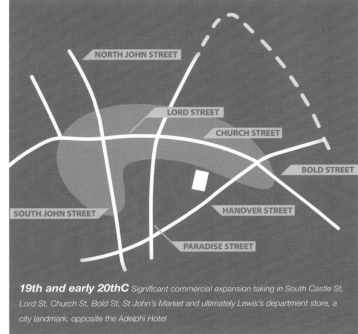

19th and early 20thC *Significant commercial expansion taking in South Castle St, Lord St, Church St, Bold St, St John's Market and ultimately Lewis's department store, a city landmark, opposite the Adelphi Hotel*

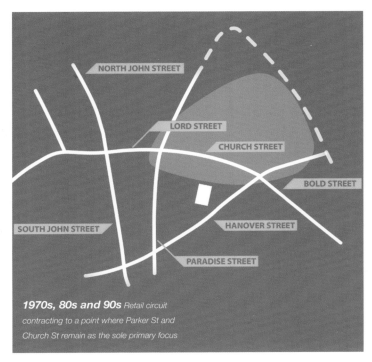

1970s, 80s and 90s *Retail circuit contracting to a point where Parker St and Church St remain as the sole primary focus*

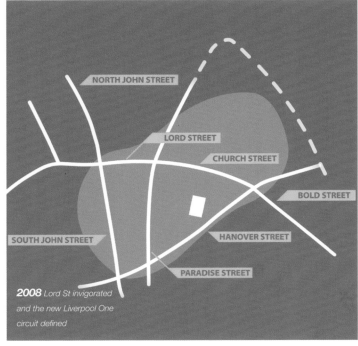

2008 *Lord St invigorated and the new Liverpool One circuit defined*

paradise lost

14 The physical environment, however, was under pressure from so much rapid expansion, so that the rather pleasant eighteenth century ambience of the place was beginning to give way to a densely packed and dirty environment. Population growth was spectacular - moving from only around 5,000 people in 1700 to almost 80,000 a century later, but mostly through in-migration rather than natural growth (morbidity rates were high). People were coming from inland, Ireland and foreign lands - drawn by the port's maritime and trade connections.

In the second half of the nineteenth century, Liverpool's prosperity was being driven primarily by its becoming a great steamship port. This tied it to economic booms in globalisation as it related to the import and export of textiles, mass migration from Europe to the Americas and the globalisation of food supplies - bulk staples as well as long-distance luxuries.

Opposite page: Top; A developed retail/street scene with open space - A busy South Castle Street looking towards the Custom House, c1907. (LRO).
Bottom; Clayton Square c1923. This and adjacent images also highlighting the city centre tram infrastructure. (Black & White Picture Place).

This page: Top left; Looking towards North John Street and junction with Lord Street (left to right). Established retail activity is evident, c1908. (LRO).
Top right; A view westwards up Lord Street, again showing this area as a popular shopping destination, c1930. (LRO).
Bottom; Lord Street/Church Street demonstrating the clearly successful economy in Liverpool at the time, c1908. (LRO).

Opposite page: Top & Bottom; Remarkable images of the 1941 wartime bomb damage following consecutive nights of air raids. The majority of historic buildings to the west of Paradise Street were destroyed in just a matter of days. (Black & White Picture Place).
This page: Bottom; Post war image of the cleared bomb sites with the demolished Custom House mid-foreground. The retained foundations define the footprint of the Old Dock. (LRO).

16   The twentieth century, however, brought wartime - and both the first and second world wars were to greatly impact on the port activities of the city. The former was the first to pose serious risks to large numbers of seamen and ships rather than simply disrupting trade routes temporarily or serving as a source for government contracts. And the latter - the Second World War - involved Liverpool playing a significant part in the subsistence of the country, acting as the chief conduit for supplies from North America. Liverpool was the headquarters of the Western Approaches Command, guiding all the convoys in and out of Britain. But it paid a heavy price, with over 80 air raids on Merseyside during the war. 'Liverpool got absolutely battered during the Blitz and the area of Paradise Street was pasted, over some very intensive raids', says Moth.

Almost the whole of the area to the west of Paradise Street was affected, with many buildings destroyed or damaged and subsequently demolished. In fact between 8th and 15th May 1941, Liverpool experienced a blitzkrieg: 2315 bombs, 119 landmines and countless incendiaries were dropped on the city. Consequently, for many years after the war the area was made up of cleared sites, half ruined buildings or ill-considered, piecemeal development that destroyed the permeability of the area. Even the important Custom House building, which had been built on the site of the old dock once it was filled in, did not escape the bombs.

cultural explosion

There had been a brief flurry of activity, however. The period following the war involved the city moving rapidly to rebuild itself after its bombardment. An entire new urban infrastructure was laid out (though never brought into reality) with modern civic buildings, shops and transport links, and the economy moved from a maritime basis to one influenced by manufacturing. As the 1950s became the 1960s, the city became a magnet for youth culture. A viable picture of the city moved from the crazed support for The Beatles - arguably the city's finest and longest-lasting export after the Fab Four had found fame in another major European port, Hamburg - to, for a short time, a booming local economy. The Merseybeat sound was forming and extending the identity of the city, worldwide. The Mersey poets followed. Tourism was consequently given a major boost and is still a large constituent of the city's economy today. In the built environment, latter-day manifestations were emerging too. The Roman Catholic Cathedral was consecrated in 1967 and the famous Anglican Cathedral was not completed until 1978.

Following the Second World War, though, the port of Liverpool went into severe decline. Many of the industries that relied on bulk processing - such as sugar and flour - went elsewhere. The heavy industrial exports from the north west of England - such as textiles and locomotives - declined, and, consequently, the local economy suffered.

But it was around this time and during the decades that followed - the 1970s and the 1980s - that Liverpool, like much of the rest of the country, went into a dark recession. Liverpool's docks and traditional manufacturing industries went into sharp decline - the advent of containerisation meant that the city's docks became largely obsolete. Then, in the early 1980s, unemployment rates in Liverpool were among the highest in the UK. The city became an unemployment black spot, and this difficult period of social problems culminated in the Toxteth riots of 1981. Originally blamed on racial tensions, it was later conceded - mainly through the Scarman report that also looked at the Brixton riots of 1980 - that wider social problems such as poverty and deprivation were part of the root cause.

Opposite page: Left; A busy
and popular Lord Street with
retail frontage all the way up
to Castle Street - trams and
cars running side by side,
c1947. (LRO).

Opposite page: Right; A
prosperous business district
with echoes of London or
even New York, with the
famous overhead railway at
the bottom of Water Street,
c1953. (Black & White Picture
Place).

This page: Top; Shanklin's
early 1960s vision for the city
centre. Constructed model,
1963 (LRO).

Bottom; The new face of
Liverpool in the early 70s.
The St John's Centre looking
from Lime St station. The
development, typical for
its era, replaced many fine
buildings including the old
market, 1973 (LRO).

20   The glimmers of a new path for the city, though, were just around the corner. And most of those glimpses of a resurrected prosperity for Liverpool came from one man: Michael - now Lord - Heseltine. According to an interview he gave the BBC in 2006, 25 years after his first involvement, Heseltine had taken three weeks off from being environment minister following the riots to see the urban deprivation for himself. Dubbed 'minister for Merseyside' and even 'Mr Merseyside', Heseltine aimed to persuade the private sector it was in their interests to help finance the regeneration of the inner city. He invited bosses of 30 significant financial institutions to take a bus ride around the area, then relaxed planning requirements and offered companies exemption from rates for industrial and commercial properties. As a result, millions of pounds' worth of investment flooded into the area. The Merseyside Development Corporation, established by Heseltine again alongside many other urban development corporations in the UK, spent over £200 million redeveloping Albert Dock and in 1984 used the International Garden Festival to bring about the regeneration of acres of derelict land. 1988's opening of Tate Liverpool further enhanced the feeling that this was a cultural city, additionally enhanced by the establishment in 1999 of the Liverpool Biennial of Contemporary Arts. More recently

still, the work of Liverpool First and then Liverpool Vision has included responsibility for redevelopment of the city centre, attempting to coordinate key private and public agencies in pursuit of wide-scale regeneration and effectively paving the way for modern 'urban living' once more.

After many false dawns, Liverpool's renaissance had finally begun.

Huge investment is now being ploughed back into a city which has a rich asset base of large, fine buildings - it has the greatest number of listed buildings outside London (2,500) and more Georgian houses than the city of Bath, for example. A brief look at a list of its finer works reveals many jewels, quite apart from the Maritime Mercantile City - now a UNESCO World Heritage site. They include Sir Frederick Gibberd's 1967 Metropolitan Cathedral of Christ the King and Sir Giles Gilbert Scott's Anglican Cathedral from the modern era, and Bluecoat Chambers - now an arts centre - from 1711 or the 1855 neoclassical St George's Hall from further back. The latter building was part of the successful bid for Liverpool as the 2008 capital of culture, acting as a springboard from the past and into the future.

Today, Liverpool is being reborn, capitalising upon its natural advantages once more and based on its historic core. Liverpool One is well placed to lead that charge.

An important period in the city's history, Heseltine's role as 'Minister for Merseyside' focuses national attention on the city's plight.

This page: *Rt Hon The Lord Heseltine.*
Opposite: *The dilapidated state of the Albert Dock through the 1970s epitomised Liverpool's sad decline and the desperate need for investment. (LRO).*

"…I would stand with a glass of wine, looking out at the magnificent view over the river, and ask myself what had gone wrong for this magnificent city'…

…'The Liver Building itself, the epicentre of a trading system that had reached out to the four corners of the earth, stood defiant and from my perspective, very alone - everything had gone wrong". Rt Hon The Lord Heseltine.

city regeneration

2

BDPs liverpool background

BDP's own involvement with Liverpool goes back several decades to the early 70s and covers a number of significant commissions. The practice's Terry Davenport vividly remembers a moment which ultimately influenced his career choice and indeed eventual position as masterplan team leader on the Liverpool One project.

'I still recall watching a classic piece of Granada TV coverage,' Davenport says, 'when local architect Ken Martin, later to become my head of school at the polytechnic, argued the case for the retention of the Albert Dock. At the time, and quite remarkably, developers proposed the wholesale demolition of the existing buildings. Ken argued his case around a beautifully set out table with 12-piece dinner service and then, towards the end of his statement, proceeded to walk around it, smashing all of the plates with a hammer! This was fairly compelling viewing and struck home, I'm sure for all who watched, the importance of protecting our heritage from the irretrievable damage of the bulldozer'.

Two years later and BDP was appointed to undertake a significant feasibility commission for relocating the myriad Liverpool Polytechnic buildings into the Albert Dock. BDP architect

director Ken Moth was a key member of the team and a previous campaigner against the docks' destruction. Although the plans did not proceed, following a narrow political vote, this first major initiative set an aspiration level for the docks' ultimate regeneration. Via Moth, BDP subsequently undertook the design of the Maritime Museum and the conversion of the Dock Traffic Office into - ironically, given Davenport's anecdote - the Granada News Headquarters during the 1980s.

Fast forward to 1998, when BDP was appointed to lead the 'Duke Street Bold Street' integrated action plan. This important study examined the regeneration framework, and particularly improved linkages, through some 90 acres of the city. Devoid of significant investment over the previous three decades, the study investigated both the Ropewalks area as it is known today, plus the ultimate Liverpool One site. Subsequently, through the emergence in 1999 of the city's retail-led regeneration brief for the Paradise Street Development Area, two crucial regeneration initiatives were defined. These areas formed the cornerstone of the city's initiatives for many years and ultimately the framework for the eventual regeneration success.

The Dock Traffic Office renovated in 1987 and converted by BDP to become Granada's new state of the art television studio. (Source unknown).

80p

Car Park

CAR
PARK
PER

Views that typified central Liverpool in the late 90s. Poor infrastructure, undeveloped post war sites, typical seventies interventions destroying permeability, little activity or investment, yet a wonderful heritage of older buildings and glimpses towards the waterfront.

Opposite; *Pre-PSDA. Examples of poor post war re-development, cluttered sightlines and unreadable streetscapes, c2004. (BDP).*

This page: Top; *A view over College Lane with Bluecoat in the foreground right and the Old Moathouse Hotel on the left, middle foreground. Note the 'dead end' visually and physically at the bottom of College Lane, c2004. (BDP).*
Right; *Typical examples of original warehouse architecture throughout the Duke Street Conservation Area. (BDP).*

The late 90s signalled a period with BDP at the heart of the city's regeneration activity. Winning the 'Duke St Bold Street integrated action plan' in 1998, the resultant report defined the overall regeneration ambition for over a hundred acres of the city centre. At the time, the city's Millennium Project was very much an ambition focused on Chavasse Park. This remained the case through the late 90s in parallel with the emerging PSDA (Paradise Street Development Area) brief for the area defined by Church Street, Hanover Street and South John Street.

The research carried out in the late 90s by Healey and Baker identified a clear shortfall of 1,000,000 ft² of prime retail space in the heart of the city centre.

This page: *Early BDP urban regeneration masterplans with PSDA boundary superimposed. (BDP).*

Opposite page: *Duke Street Conservation Area - 'Ropewalks' - Regeneration. (BDP).*

i) Movement & connectivity between the city and the new Ropewalks areas, including the Bluecoat Triangle.

ii) Masterplanning; Zoned uses and activities.

duke street
bold street

integrated action plan

Concert square

Concert Square has been the most successful piece of urban regeneration within the Duke Street/Bold Street area and it continues to expand and attract further people into this part of the city.

The area identified is currently dominated by night-time and bar/restaurant uses. Retail, residential and some existing industrial uses also exist in the area. Looking to the future, there are many things that still need to be done if that success story is to continue, and grow.

A number of buildings have been identified where redevelopment is required and the change in existing uses can also be justified through further development of bar/restaurant uses at ground floor and redevelopment of upper stories for office/workspace use.

Concert Square attracts many people, particularly at night. Streets get congested and access is difficult by car and environmentally the area is not as appealing as it should be. Wide ranging environmental improvements are therefore proposed in this area, particularly to improve the streetscape, lighting and overall safety so that other people can feel comfortable within this busy vibrant, buzzing environment.

In the longer term, it is quite possible to perceive the retail uses, currently contained within Bold Street and Hanover Street, permeating through into Concert Square, Fleet Street, Wood Street and extending the exciting shopping environment emerging in the Bold Street area. The redevelopment of the Hanover Street car park at the bottom of Seel Street in the longer term will provide a valuable off street parking resource.

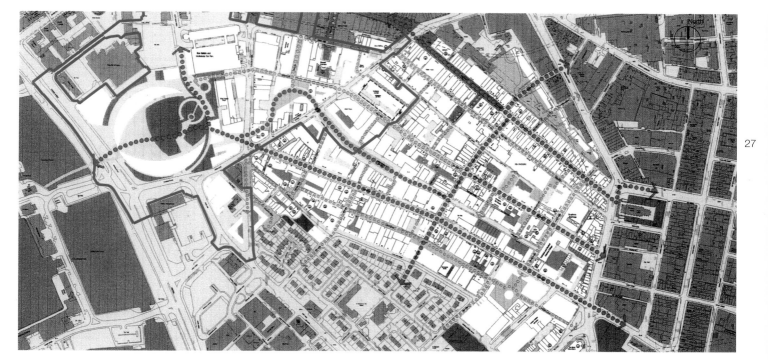

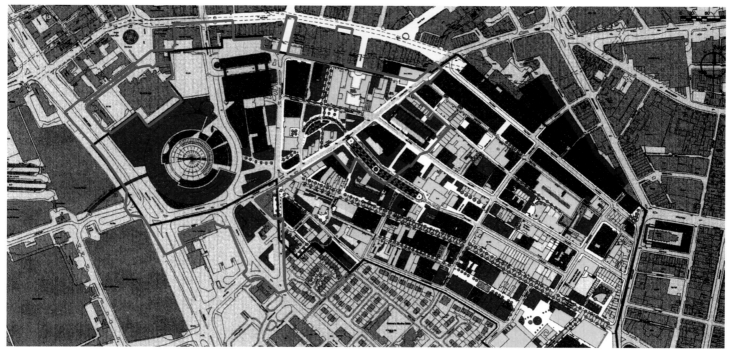

28 **This page: Top;** Campbell Square - public realm including street art by Brock Carmichael Architects. **Bottom;** BDP's public realm in St Peter's Square; one of several new public spaces created in BDP's regeneration plan for Ropewalks.

Opposite page: Successful urban regeneration - Concert Square.

BDP's commitment to the Ropewalks regeneration continued through the masterplanning, design and delivery of the new routes and public spaces, including St Peter's Square, between 1999 and 2004. Urban Splash's first development a few years earlier in Concert Square signalled the enormous potential.

competition & development brief

30   But that success relied on an important initial aspiration. When the Paradise Street project was first being considered as a large-scale regeneration scheme, the fundamental principle was that this should not be a shopping mall just dropped onto the site. Instead, it should take the street pattern and few surviving historic buildings along College Lane, School Lane and Hanover Street - such as the Grade I-listed Bluecoat Chambers and small warehouses behind it - and integrate them into the wider vision. That lost permeability should be regained and it should, it was felt, be more of a recreation of the city centre based on the historic street patterns, with a variety of buildings that celebrate the historic core of the city. This, essentially, is what has been built.

'The development now stitches together what was the surviving commercial core of Liverpool very logically into the new Paradise Street development,' says Moth, 'and it links very well into the Ropewalks area and the old Georgian port of Liverpool. I think the principles have worked well, and the fact that it was recreating a city block based on the old historic streets has allowed a variety of architects to come in and design individual buildings, so you have got that variety of authorship and building expressions. They are important to a city centre.'

retail therapy

In many ways, Liverpool One has met a need, both in terms of the city and the north-west region as a whole. But beyond satisfying the retail requirements of a shopping community, it has also acted to regenerate a whole quarter,

reconnecting it to the waterfront once more. The competition and development brief was where this process began. Once upon a time, says former Liverpool council leader Mike Storey - now head teacher at Plantation Primary School in the city - Liverpool used to be a 'premier retail destination'. 'I think it was in the top four of retail destinations and it went through quite a singular decline for all sorts of social and economic reasons', he says. Added to this picture was the political dimension, where government legislation allowed a boom in out-of-town retailing opportunities, throwing up rival developments such as the Trafford Centre and swinging the commercial pendulum Manchester's way. Furthermore, despite a 'town centres first' policy from government, retail in many UK city centres was - and is - still finding it tough.

What was needed was a 'step change', to bring Liverpool's centre up to scratch, to outshine local rivals and prove worthy of a major European city.

'We looked at retailing and said we needed to do something about this', Storey recalls, 'so we brought in Healey & Baker to look at the whole retailing issue.'

The specialist consultant's main conclusions then, in the late 1990s, were that, first of all, Liverpool needed to grow its retailing offer. Secondly though, cites Storey, in doing that, the council and other interested parties needed to be careful to avoid weakening the city's central retail provision. In other words, locating the development was a delicate issue. The kinds of shops on offer would also be important in order to lift the tone. Storey again: '[The Healey & Baker report] also said that retailing had

become very, very cheap - it was more at the bottom end of the market, more for younger people, less for affluent shoppers and there wasn't the variety, particularly in fashion.'

Liverpool Vision chief executive Jim Gill says this retail plan was crucial, and became embodied into the strategic regeneration framework of his organisation - the UK's first urban regeneration company.

But that location issue was a key driver. This was highlighted by other factors. For example, when Storey became leader in 1998, there was a proposal from developers called Intercity to develop King's Dock. Storey's council rejected it because it was thought that this might draw too many shoppers away from the centre and only serve to help kill it off. Healey & Baker was asked to look at possible locations, and came up with the location bounded by Hanover Street, School Lane, College Lane and Chavasse Park. At the time, this was called the Paradise Street Development Area, or PSDA. The report, in short, had gone down well. Storey again: 'We embraced everything Healey & Baker said - it seemed to make sense to us, an extra two million square feet of retail.'

The next step was to get developers interested in taking the proposal forward. In 1999 the competition for the site was launched and drew a surprisingly 'blue-chip' set of names. Seven made the cut from the initial tranche. Hammerson, Multi Development Corporation, Capital Shopping Centres, Lendlease/Land Securities, Westfield, Peel Holdings and Grosvenor/Henderson were shortlisted. (As an aside, Storey says he was even offered an all expenses paid trip by Westfield to fly out and view some of the firm's work in Australia - which he obviously declined, citing the UK's tighter regulations on such matters.)

But it was apparent that the council was clear-sighted in its objectives from the outset, always a help from a client body to any development programme.

'We made some very strict rules about what we wanted', Storey says, 'We said we did not want a giant mall under any circumstances. Giant malls were out. We wanted to use existing street patterns and we wanted also to ensure that listed buildings and buildings of significance were kept. We wanted to work with local architects on schemes, we wanted to try and develop and link the waterfront with the new retail area.'

Part of this motivation was against the mall principle and in favour of the notion that cities are about an all-weather experience. So the council remained obdurately against malls, even during the developer selection process, when they were urged many times to reconsider. Partially this pressure from the developers was because, to some of those firms, the mall process might have been a good degree simpler and cheaper. Storey, though, wanted the 'hustle and bustle' of a New York or a Dublin, and feels vindicated today that he chose the right direction. 'It's one of those moments where I'm proud we stuck to our guns'.

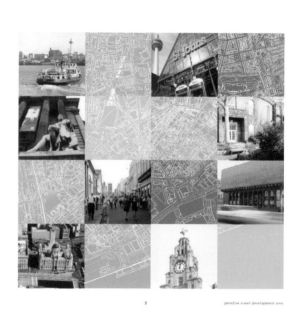

bluecoat

paradise street development area

A submission to
Liverpool City Council

August 1999

Above: Produced by BDP, the cover of Grosvenor's original 'expression of interest' to Liverpool City Council in response to the PSDA development brief. One of over 30 submissions made to the Council in August 99 by major national and international developers. (BDP).

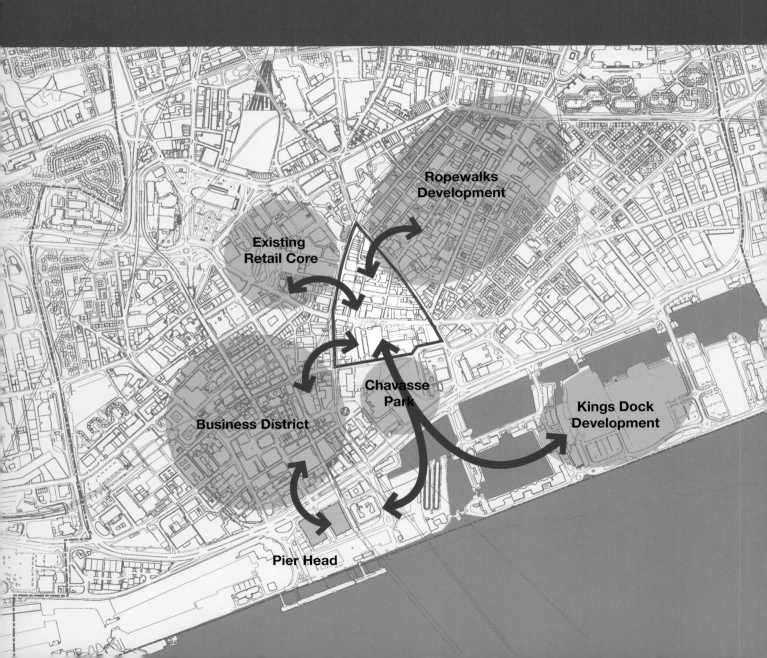

Ropewalks Development

Existing Retail Core

Business District

Chavasse Park

Kings Dock Development

Pier Head

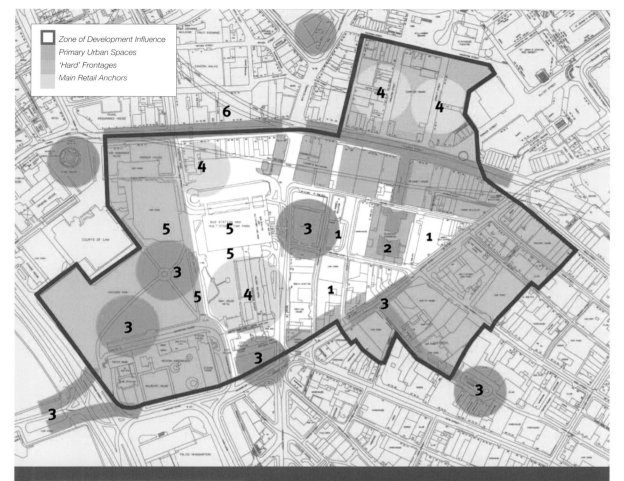

Zone of Development Influence
Primary Urban Spaces
'Hard' Frontages
Main Retail Anchors

This page and opposite: Extracts from the submission documents. (BDP).

Opposite page: Zones of influence, analysis of city districts. (BDP).

This page: Bottom left; Liverpool Vision's core strategy for the city's regeneration drivers.

1 Smaller retail/mixed use elements responding to Rope Walks scale.
2 Bluecoat Chambers.
3 Necklace of quality urban spaces created linking Ropewalks & Kings Dock.
4 Main retail anchors.
5 Core retail elements potentially on more than 1 level in part.
6 Reinforce linkages with Mathew Street & Cavern Walks. New Department Store strengthens Lord Street.
  • New civic space created at heart of scheme.
  • Development proposals and masterplan must address weakening secondary retail north of Church Street.
  • Need to consider dedicated service & parking access serving below ground to both Paradise Street and Chavasse Park sites.

34 **This page:** *Early concept sketches showing potential cityscapes. (BDP).*
Top; *Looking towards junction of Lord Street and Castle Street from Queen Elizabeth Law Courts. (BDP).*
Middle; *Riverside view with Liverpool One to the right.*
Bottom; *View from the Strand looking up to the head of the park. (BDP).*

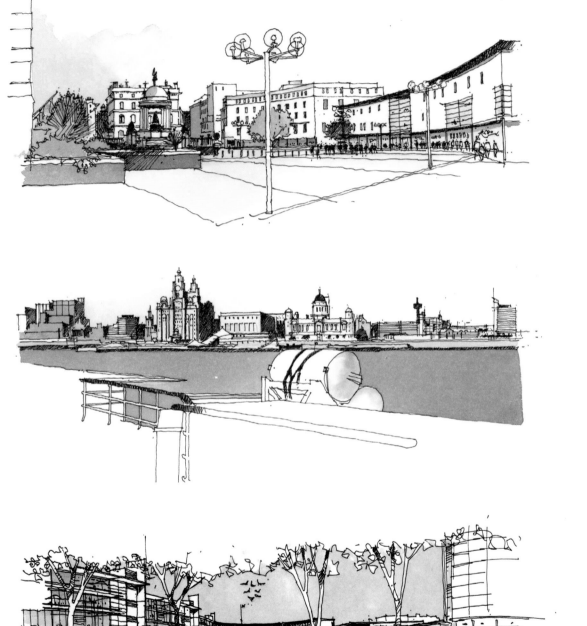

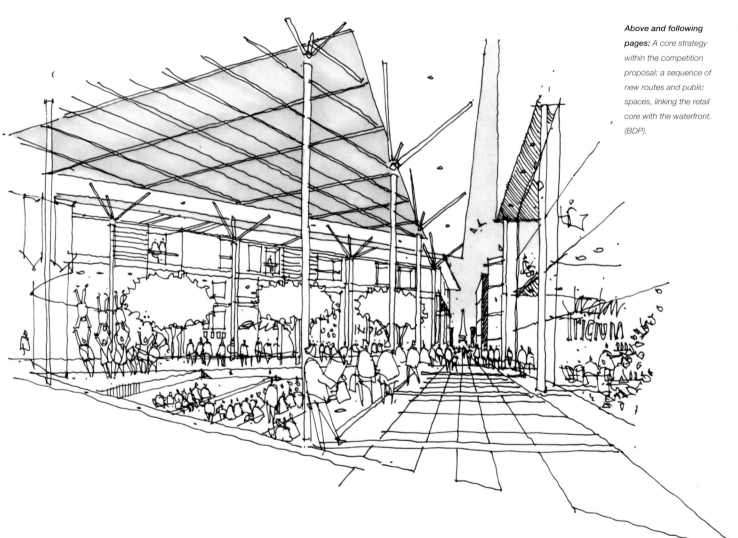

Above and following pages: *A core strategy within the competition proposal; a sequence of new routes and public spaces, linking the retail core with the waterfront. (BDP).*

36 **This page: Top;** *Looking back towards School Lane from a new 'triangular space' in the heart of the 'Bluecoat Triangle'. (BDP).*

This page: Bottom; *Looking across new Paradise Place towards the waterfront. (BDP).*

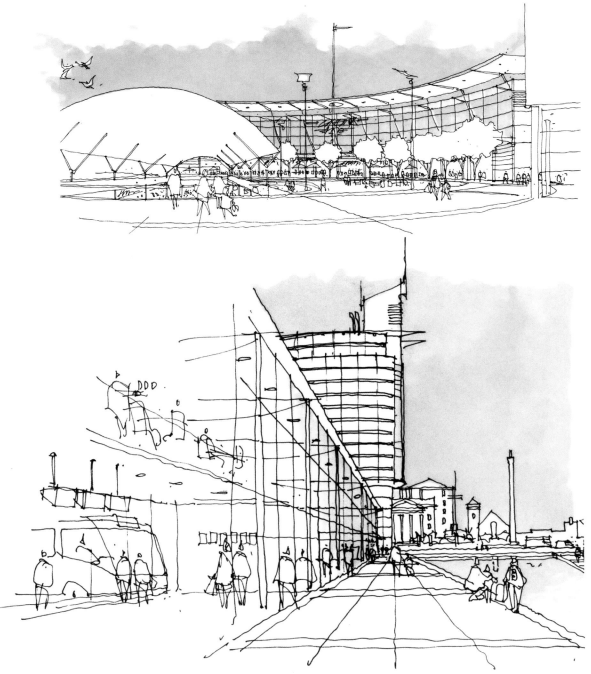

This page: The early vision of the leisure focus at the head of the park, single level South John Street to the left. Remarkably similar to the final Liverpool One layout. (BDP).

Below; Looking along Thomas Steers Way (Discovery Axis) over the Strand to the Pump House Pub and Albert Dock. (BDP).

Following page: the original 6 panel competition submission. A comprehensive vision for the integration of this major project into the heart of the city. (BDP).

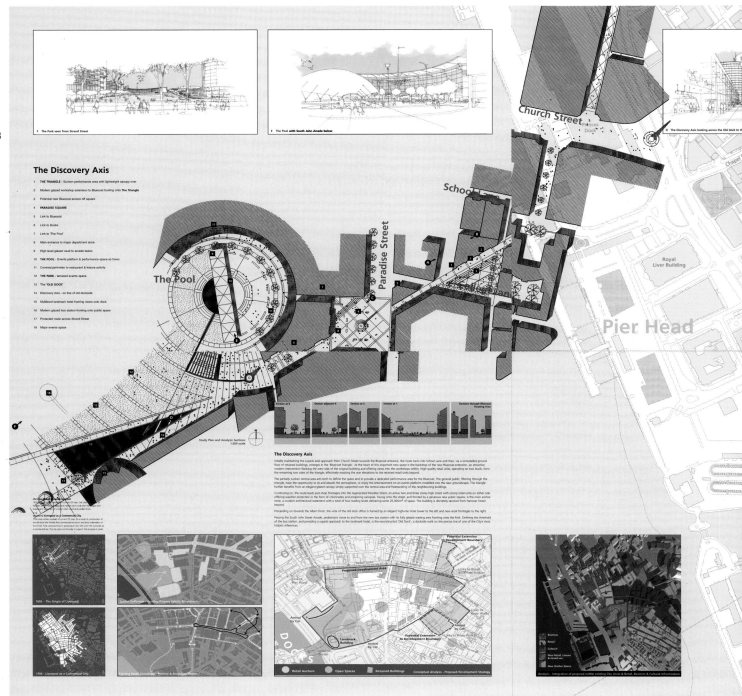

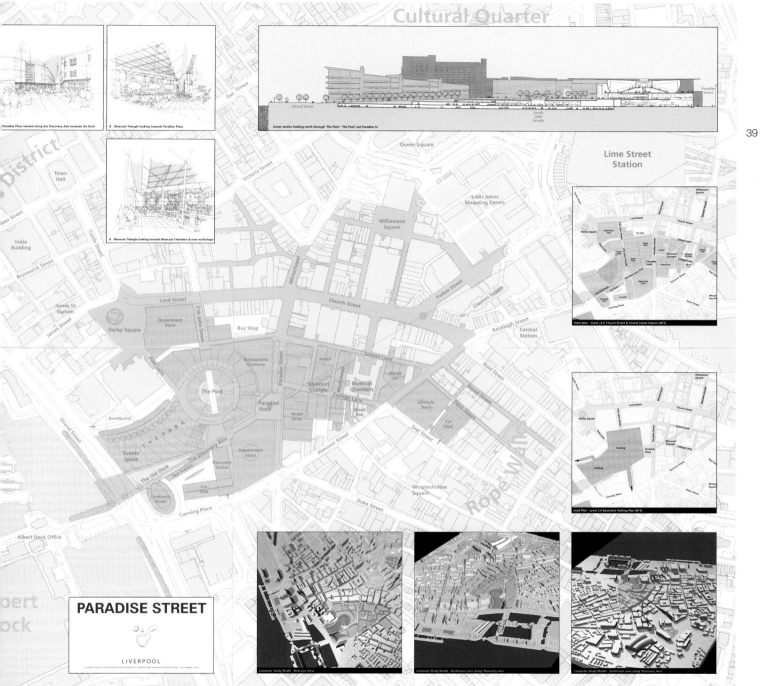

A Paradise Place viewed along the Discovery Axis towards the Dock

B Bluecoat Triangle looking towards Paradise Place

A Bluecoat Triangle looking towards Bluecoat Chambers & new workshops

Linear section looking north through 'The Park', 'The Pool' and Paradise St

Lime Street Station

Inset plan - Level +6.0 Church Street & Strand Street Datum (NTS)

Inset Plan - Level 3.0 Basement Parking Plan (NTS)

PARADISE STREET

LIVERPOOL

Computer Study Model - Birds Eye View

Computer Study Model - Northwest view along 'Discovery Axis'

Computer Study Model - Southwest view along 'Discovery Axis'

'I think it's made a huge difference', he says. 'Never mind the whole issue of thousands of jobs during the construction, there are also thousands of jobs in retail and management and leisure that have been created. And I think the scheme for the first time ever has actually linked the waterfront with the city centre.'

former Liverpool council leader Mike Storey

local heroes

Local voices were clearly an important factor, right from the beginning, and early instincts about the correct way forward would prove decisive. As a born and bred Liverpudlian, BDP's Terry Davenport is proud to have played a leading role in the development. 'I was involved from the first day of the project and vividly recall sitting down with John Bullough at Grosvenor in an oak panelled room to discuss the strategy for the development competition. It was an exciting time, and we quickly established a template to take the initial expression of interest forward. The core principles of the scheme - a triangular retail circuit, an intervention onto Lord Street, a sequence of public spaces, strong linkages, the principle of undercroft parking, the aspect of the sites, fine buildings and streetscape - were all established in the first few weeks of our thinking.'

Following Grosvenor's shortlisting, work continued apace on the competition submission during autumn 1999, with Rod Holmes joining the team in October. Needless to say, it was a fairly intensive period with pressure on all fronts given the significance of the project.

The shortlist was whittled down to four, after which there was an appraisal from officers and elected members. Then it was down to two - Hammerson and Grosvenor. In the end the panel was split on the decision and - surprisingly - not along party lines. Storey's casting vote sealed it for Grosvenor, but only after much thorough discussion and debate and a clear-the-head walk with David Henshaw, the then chief executive of Liverpool City Council. Storey again: 'He said to me, "what do you want, Mike?" and I said, "I just feel that the chemistry is right - I'm terribly impressed with what Hammerson wants to do but I just think the chemistry is right with Grosvenor".'

Other 'local' connections may also have helped, with Grosvenor former executive chairman the Duke of Westminster's home across the way in Cheshire. But in the end, after much more discussion, the panel had voted unanimously for Grosvenor. 'And they have been everything we hoped they would be', Storey says. 'All the way through the process, we set up a members' working group of four or five members, and with each development the architects have come and presented and we've looked at buildings.'

Liverpool Vision had opted for Grosvenor too, says Gill, mostly through the then chairman Sir Joe Dwyer, shortly before Gill arrived on the scene. 'Joe always said that his recommendation to the city was to go with Grosvenor because of the nature of them as a company', he says. 'I think they were really selected on the basis of an approach, which was broadly one of "we'll work with you to create a quality retail location in the centre of the city".'

Liverpool Vision's role was, in Gill's words, to keep a watching brief, helping to sort issues as they arose, and hosting visits for investors with Grosvenor. 'What I think Grosvenor got out of that was that here was a city centre that had a clear plan, and had a commitment through an urban regeneration company', says Gill. The tri-partite arrangement of the city council, regional development agency and English Partnerships could offer a powerful context for investment. 'It gave Grosvenor confidence', says Gill, 'and Grosvenor was able to transfer that confidence through to their investment partners.'

Throughout the ensuing early processes the engagement between members, Grosvenor and the architects was 'amazing' and unprecedented, believes Storey, with the team using design analysis and workshop sessions to determine five key objectives. These were essentially to: differentiate the development area from other parts of the city and other cities in the UK; provide a robust framework to enable architecture and landscape design of the highest quality; be inclusive to the needs of all; and to take a comprehensive approach to the regeneration of the area and its integration into the city centre.

BDP worked hard on analysis diagrams to set principles for the masterplan, evolving into a vision of different 'quarters' within the scheme, but all integrated with the existing fabric of the city.

The result has also impressed Storey, with, he believes, far-reaching implications for the city's status.

'I think it's made a huge difference', he says. 'Never mind the whole issue of thousands of jobs during the construction, there are also thousands of jobs in retail and management and leisure that have been created. And I think for the first time ever the scheme has actually linked the waterfront with the city centre.'

Gill agrees, calling the process 'an exemplary way to go about things'. The approach to working, creating a 'shared vision for what the area should be about', was a strong one. 'The masterplanning process was one that engaged a lot of people and engaged the public', says Gill. 'Very importantly, it engaged not just professionals in the city council but members as well.' The process set a clear agenda with regular, frequent meetings that brought about a real dialogue. 'You could say that the masterplan and the key elements that make up the masterplan - which was the way the retail area was structured - were the results of very real engagement', Gill adds. 'Not just consultation, but very real engagement.'

This has led to 'stupendous, spectacular', high quality - and long-lasting - results for the city, replacing a scruffy, scrappy local environment, and helping to shift the centre of gravity closer to the waterfront. 'In terms of the physical fabric of the city centre and therefore what it's offering, Liverpool has caught up with most of what it's missed in the last 40 years', says Gill.

Allied to the developments at the pier head and the new museum, and to King's Dock, Liverpool One's competition process and development brief has created linkage and prosperity, even beyond figures originally predicted by Liverpool's successful European Capital of Culture bid, which foresaw an extra 1.7 million tourists and the creation of an extra 11,000 jobs. 'We've exceeded those figures dramatically', says Storey. 'It's a good story to tell the kids.'

'The masterplanning process was one that engaged a lot of people and engaged the public', says Gill. 'Very importantly, it engaged not just professionals in the city council but members as well.'

'You could say that the masterplan and the key elements that make up the masterplan - which was the way the retail area was structured - were the results of very real engagement', Gill adds. 'Not just consultation but very real engagement.'

masterplan
evolution

3

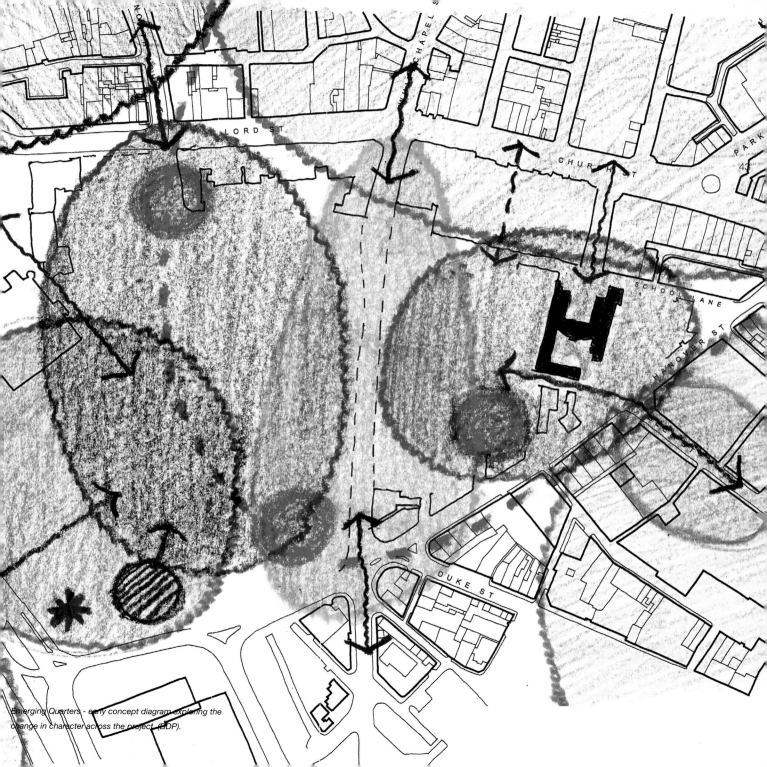

Emerging Quarters - early concept diagram exploring the change in character across the project. (BDP).

masterplan evolution

44 Developing the masterplan for Liverpool One lay at the very heart of forging its success as a place - a seamless reconstruction of the city, rather than a corporate, gated, no-go zone after dark.

BDP was central to this process, working to harness the different architects together and melding the development's different quarters and atmospheres - using a viable city-building ethos based on urban blocks, streets, spaces, views and no little sense of delight.

Rod Holmes, the Grosvenor director held in high regard by all concerned with the emerging scheme, recalls the starting point for the masterplan was a background of the new urban agenda and Lord Rogers' report, Towards an Urban Renaissance. 'We had also been talking about thinking again about shopping centres as we moved back out of the 90s recession', he says. 'We began to think that maybe we should start from scratch, as it were, to think afresh about what shopping environments were like.'

It helped that Liverpool City Council had given Grosvenor a high-quality brief to aid this process, emphasising the importance of good linkages into the adjacent areas of the city. 'That was one of their requirements, and they used the word 'permeability'', says Holmes.

The brief stemmed from the Healey & Baker retail report, as we have seen, and it was the view of Grosvenor, BDP and the city that the resulting project should try to use the street pattern, rather than fight it. Rather than create new forms, it should work with the grain of the city. Partially this view stemmed from Holmes' own experience of working in places like The Hague in Holland, but it was also something of an instinct about the map of Liverpool and the realisation that things radiated from the spot where the city sprang from - the Pool and the dock. 'I had a gut feeling that in the 50s, 60s, 70s and 80s', says Holmes, 'wherever we'd buggered around with the old street pattern, we'd almost always got it wrong; we ended up with weird streets that didn't go anywhere. It generally created funny situations in cities.'

One such odd scenario was the development of the St John's Centre in Liverpool, with its rear facing one of the great neoclassical buildings of Europe, St George's Hall. Holmes embarked with BDP leading the masterplan team, having developed the schematic principles during autumn 1999 in the first round of the competition. Going forward, it was a case of working with the city from first principles - assessing people's aspirations and questioning afresh. This was around November 1999. BDP urbanism director Richard Rees says a lot of work by himself and Terry Davenport went into preparing the bedrock for the masterplan to progress in what was, looking back, a crucial period. By early 2000, Holmes remembers, a general arrangement for the proposed development had been arrived at, and the early months of that year were spent honing and working this up, starting with the street pattern, trying to create viable shopping circuits, working to get a good, vertical mix of users. It was also spent locating particular developments in the wider scheme in the right positions, along with public transport facilities and parking.

In April of 2000, Rees and BDP chief executive Peter Drummond joined the team for the critical next six months of the masterplan stage. The main problem at this time, recalls Rees, was that the design was not producing enough retail space. The competition had worked well in terms of creating the right atmosphere and feel, but it did not appear to do the job in terms of sheer numbers. 'Myself, Peter Drummond and Terry got together for that period and went back to first principles on the masterplan', says Rees, 'and the little scribbly sketch of making the connections and the regional circuits work on the site was actually the critical one in terms of bringing the concept forward.'

The other main move was to make South John Street a two-level space, a substantial change at that point and potentially significant for the character of the whole development. Rees again: 'What we were trying to do was draw people south from Church Street downwards and we were trying to get them to experience a variety of different spaces.' At this point, regular working sessions were being held with the city's team, in particular Healey & Baker, to thoroughly test a wide variety of two-level solutions in order to maximise value.

Moves were made to bring distinct characters to different areas, largely drawing on the historic buildings in those areas and the network of streets around Hanover Street. This had the effect of pulling people through, whilst the masterplanners had to simultaneously make allowances for things like an early tram proposal down Paradise Street. As it turned out, this was something which never materialised, although the capacity is still there if the concept is revisited. Another constraint was on height, especially around Bluecoat, and the designation of World Heritage Site status. Both created a sensitivity with English

Heritage on scale and other matters.

Following a hectic Christmas period, the hybrid planning application, contained within dozens of large cardboard boxes, was submitted to the city council. Design development and consultations, not least with Mersey Travel, continued through 2001. By this time the eastern side of the development, with its six detailed applications, was getting there, but to the west of Paradise Street much work still had to be done. 'Then we had a workshop', says Holmes. 'I guess it was the spring of 2001, where we invited Terry Farrell, Rafael Viñoly and Cesar Pelli.' This workshop was held in the Athenaeum with the three world famous architects, brainstorming - principally concerning the western side - in a bid to try to resolve it in urban design terms. But it also grappled with other questions. How could the waterfront be dealt with? How about the Strand? At this stage, people were still talking about the possibility of bridging over the main thoroughfare. Holmes recalls how BDP director of architecture Terry Davenport reaffirmed an important notion at around this point. 'His expression was the 'discovery axis' - a direct line of sight and pedestrian movement between the pediment of the old Granada Studio on the Albert Dock and the core of our development in this triangle. That expression, 'discovery axis', stretched for a long time until we eventually renamed it Thomas Steers Way after the engineer who designed the Old Dock.'

Pelli's firm, Pelli Clarke Pelli Architects, was selected to work on the project, principally because, as Holmes relates, it was felt that they had done more analysis than Farrell or Viñoly. 'They had pointed out to us that

there was a slight kink in the alignment of the Mersey, and that resulted in a different set of urban grids, the very rigid grid of the Three Graces waterfront from James Street and then the much more complex arrangement of the alignment of the streets around the Ropewalks.' Pelli came up with the idea of resolving them by using an elliptical shape and then, later on, another inside, with the second ellipse on the ground being the shape of the park. The park was an ambiguous space because it was both ground and roof, says Rees, and forms a side to a street as well as being an edge to the park. Critically at this stage, Davenport recalls, the agreement with Mersey Travel to relocate the bus interchange to Canning Place unlocked a number of previously challenging restrictions.

All the while, though, the masterplan sought to retain the compactness of the city. The model for South John Street, with its two big department stores, emanated from recognised European examples. Rees points to very clear examples of the Netherlands experience and the benefits that it brought to the wider project. 'The Dutch lesson was that you could create an intense retail environment using streets as opposed to an enclosed space', he says. It was also a mission to get as much variety and spatial quality onto the project as possible, so that it was really a city experience, rather than an architectural one. As it reached its endgame, the project was built largely to the original masterplan. And the point about a good masterplan is that it sets the parameters at just the right level, Rees adds. 'We had to get those parameters so the architects could deal with the blocks they were given in just the right manner, and not restrict

them too far', he says. 'The masterplan should be a neutral stage where you keep a bucketful of opportunities available for you to develop further.' By contrast, a poor masterplan is one which is overly deterministic, and sets too many stringent codes.

Over on the eastern end of the scheme, meanwhile, development plans involved debates about whether Grosvenor should, as was originally intended, use Church Alley, the street in front of the Bluecoat Chambers where it connects into Church Street. Should this part be used as a linkage back into Church Street opposite Marks and Spencer? Ultimately this meant acquiring an old Top Shop/HMV building, a move resisted by Grosvenor for some time. 'It was the only way we could get enough depth on both sides of what became Peter's Lane', says Holmes. 'With the arcade, we needed trading on both sides of Peter's Lane.' The move was challenged, but emerged victorious, at public inquiry.

Sightlines to important buildings were also an important part of the emerging picture, with Terry Davenport a key driver of this process, particularly with regard to the Liver Building from along College Lane and another glimpse from School Lane. Another was to maintain views of the pediment on Albert Dock. Later, one of Holmes' own interventions was to install a small view 'scoop' to allow views of the cupola on Bluecoat. Similarly, views of the Anglican Cathedral are protected as much as possible. BDP established all of these sightlines as an integral - and important - part of the masterplan. 'As a result, you know exactly where you are in Liverpool', says Rees of these sightline orientation devices. None of the streets is the same width and each

46 building has a different set of grids, again contributing to a feeling of surprise and delight, he adds. The Liverpool One scheme as a whole is largely informal, with the park's oval and the axis of discovery the only semblances of formality.

Permeability was of course the other main strand, and that key early requirement from the city council. Holmes is a firm believer that Liverpool One had to be a part of the city. 'We always knew that we would have to connect it absolutely, seamlessly, without gates, barriers, revolving doors - anything', he says. 'We would have to be open contiguously with the existing shopping area. People now are not entirely sure where one begins, and that is how it should be.'

Trevor Skempton, formerly head of architecture at Birmingham University, was brought in to help in an urban design role on the City Centre Development Team, pushing to bring forth some of the principles on urban design that were then being espoused and adopted by the Commission for Architecture and the Built Environment (CABE) and others. Skempton relates another interesting anecdote about linkages on the project. The 'zig-zag' stair came about through pretty unusual circumstances. The feature occurs on the Allies and Morrison-designed building at Liverpool One. Initially the masterplan had proposed a cut at that point, and Allies and Morrison's early proposal was for twin escalators with a staircase up each side, drawing on examples in Lisbon and in Montmartre in Paris. But, recalls Skempton, the building inspector, Keith Bold, intervened. 'It wasn't his remit because it is an external staircase, but he was asked about it and said, "well, I'm afraid, it may be all right in Lisbon or in Montmartre but in Liverpool on a Friday night, with a night-time economy, people tripping up and down from the park down toward the Ropewalks... it's just not on. You need to have not only landings every so often but a change of direction on the landings".'

The architect took it on board and another feature was born. 'But it's a landmark that's not contrived', says Skempton. 'That's the nice thing about it. It's actually arisen out of a collective process.' It was also a good symbol that debate had clearly led to concerns, which had led in turn to a speedy and stylish response. And, as Rees emphasises, it showed that the masterplan was not a restriction on creativity.

Permeability as a whole is successful insofar as Liverpool One basically faces in all directions, says Skempton again. 'And within the scheme there is enough complexity so people can wander – they don't have to follow a prescribed retail triangle or prescribed route. They can wander around and then they're never quite sure when they're in Liverpool One and when they're in the rest of the city.'

It was also quite a move, says Rees, to break through a building on South Church Street after experimenting with different diagonals. The layering of the site makes it possible to go up and over buildings as well as through them, and there are thresholds and belvederes throughout the site because of that.

As highlighted, the decision to go to a system of multi-level shopping was another key point in the development of the masterplan. Rees points to a contretemps with CABE about the use of escalators in streets, which the commission viewed as non-natural methods of movement that were too mall-like. Holmes admits he struggled with going multi-level, and points to Healey & Baker as having driven the importance of the issue home as a way of trying to get more value out of the site. 'When we originally started discussions with the council, there wasn't enough residual left over at the end of the costs against the value to assemble the site', he explains. 'So, all the time we had to add value. The scheme grew and joined course with those discussions.'

Skempton points out that it is only

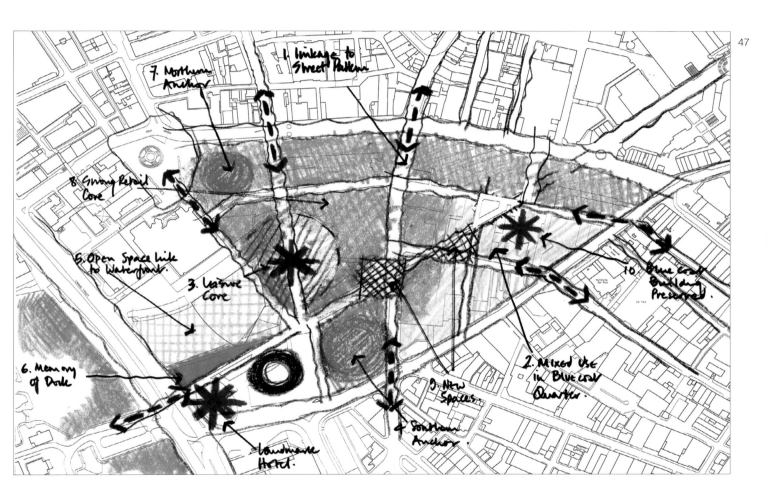

1. linkage to Street Pattern

7. Northern Anchor

8. Strong Retail Core

5. Open Space link to Waterfront.

3. Leisure Core

6. Memory of Dock

Landmark Hotel.

9. New Spaces.

4. Southern Anchor.

2. Mixed use in Blue coat Quarter.

10. Blue coat Building Preserved.

Above: The first steps – initial development of the competition proposals and statement of core objectives. (BDP).

two retail levels, and both John Lewis and Debenhams can be accessed at both. 'It's quite cleverly done by BDP that both levels merge effortlessly into ground at one end or the other', he says. Perhaps, though, there was an even more subtle dimension to this multi-levelled approach, too? 'I think there was a conscious attempt here, on that particular street, to reference the shopping mall', Skempton believes. 'It's almost like an ironic reference, even though we're all trying to get away from the mall.'

Permeability is improved by the Castle Mound end of the project to the north-west, says Rees, aiding the way people can feed into the scheme at different levels. The big blocks needed to be overcome, and Rees believes this has been achieved, with the masterplan resulting in a very 'celebratory scheme' in the way it ushers people around.

The mix of uses - shopping, leisure and residential - is also an important constituent in urban design terms, since as you link such uses, you make them permeable, and thereby increase activity. 'People have been persuaded that a healthy slice of city is going to be a good place to be', says Skempton. 'I think in that sense, BDP has done very well, and has accepted that there are compromises in it. But I think the permeability is good.'

The process of getting the best from the many different architects contributing their designs to the whole Liverpool One project masterplan was another important element in achieving what the masterplan laid out as a series of objectives. For each building, the masterplan team provided a comprehensive brief. After that, each design as it got past preliminary stages went under the noses of the council leader, senior council politicians, and workshops involving Grosvenor and its equity partners; anybody, in fact, that Holmes felt might have something useful to say about what was being shown. This became the Thursday review. Every Thursday morning, designs were reviewed at different stages, starting with the member working group and architects talking about their schemes and the wider Liverpool picture. It was a good, iterative process, involving Holmes, Davenport, other BDP colleagues, contractors and others. 'They were almost invariably good-natured, well-structured', says Holmes, and they often included quantity surveyors talking about design issues, alongside girls from the information centre offering their views. 'For me they were the most enjoyable, most successful, most stimulating part of the whole process', says Holmes. The public meetings where Grosvenor and BDP presented their plans were similarly provoking, enlightening and productive.

The masterplan proved robust and flexible enough to be challenged, too, says Trevor Skempton, since it allowed space for buildings of a maverick nature, such as Piers Gough's (CZWG) 'Bling Bling' building for hairdresser Herbert, a flamboyant Liverpool character. This was a rehousing of a building that was within Paradise Street, and on the strength of his performance here Gough was invited back to compete for another on the site (which eventually went to Glen Howells Architects). 'What we were trying to do', says Rees, 'was create a matrix of opportunity. And that's what we did.'

Ultimately, the lesson of the masterplan to Skempton has been that the extraordinary complexity of having so many architects and design teams involved will be rewarded, both the for the developer and the city, in the long term. 'Because what they don't want is for the the thing to become obsolete again in 30 or 40 years and have another cycle of renewal. Liverpool doesn't need that. Cities don't need that, on this scale. And I think they've a really good chance that this is a graft into the city that will take.'

Rees agrees. Liverpool One's main success, and the enduring success of the masterplan, is that 'it doesn't feel like something that's been applied to the city in a big, gestural way. It feels like what it should be', he says, 'which is a mixture of different types and designs of buildings.' It is also, he believes, lifting Liverpool's standing on a European scale up several notches.

But perhaps the main secret to achieving the masterplan's key principles, however, has been having a committed design champion to see it through. Trevor Skempton is full of praise for Holmes' management style. 'Rod Holmes was a champion of quite extraordinary tenacity', he says. 'I can't praise that element of Rod's work enough. Rod's a control freak, which can be an unattractive quality. But his sophistication in approaching and dealing with architects was extraordinary.'

Holmes himself agrees that large scale projects do need a focus. 'You always need one or two - usually one person - who is obsessive', he says. 'And slightly unhinged.'

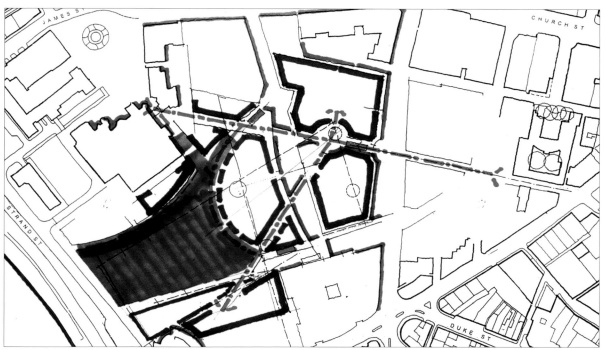

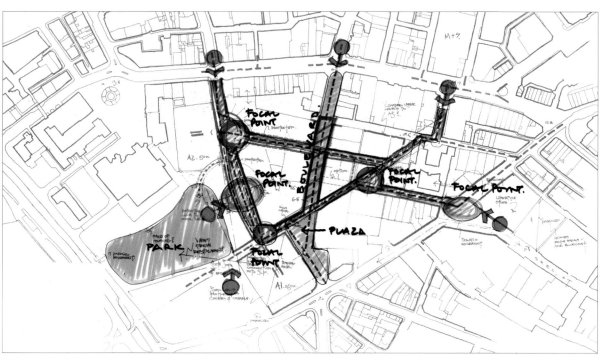

This page: Countless development studies were undertaken to explore the developing masterplan and, in particular, the connectivity between the emerging proposals and existing city context. (BDP).

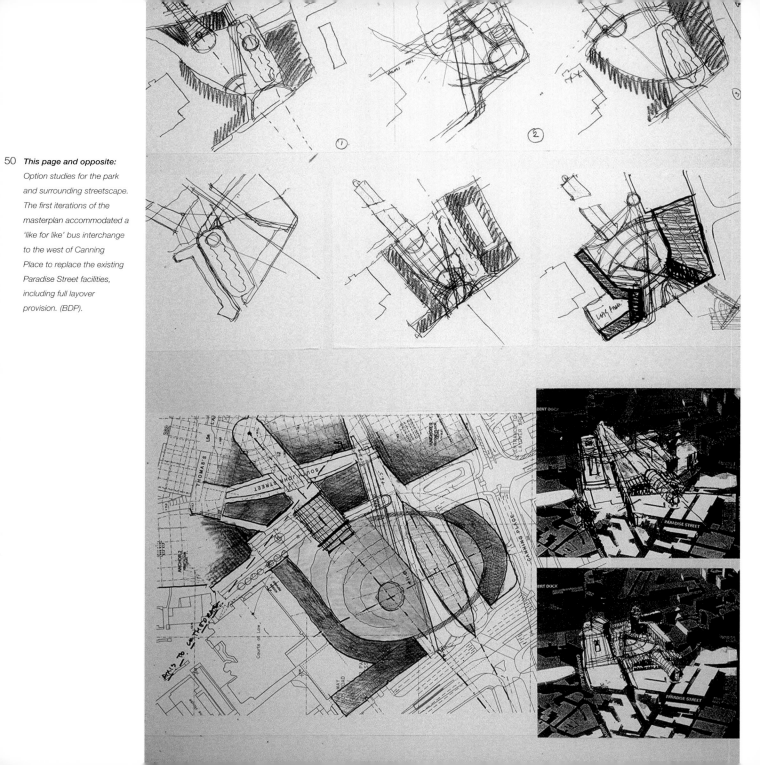

50 **This page and opposite:**
Option studies for the park
and surrounding streetscape.
The first iterations of the
masterplan accommodated a
'like for like' bus interchange
to the west of Canning
Place to replace the existing
Paradise Street facilities,
including full layover
provision. (BDP).

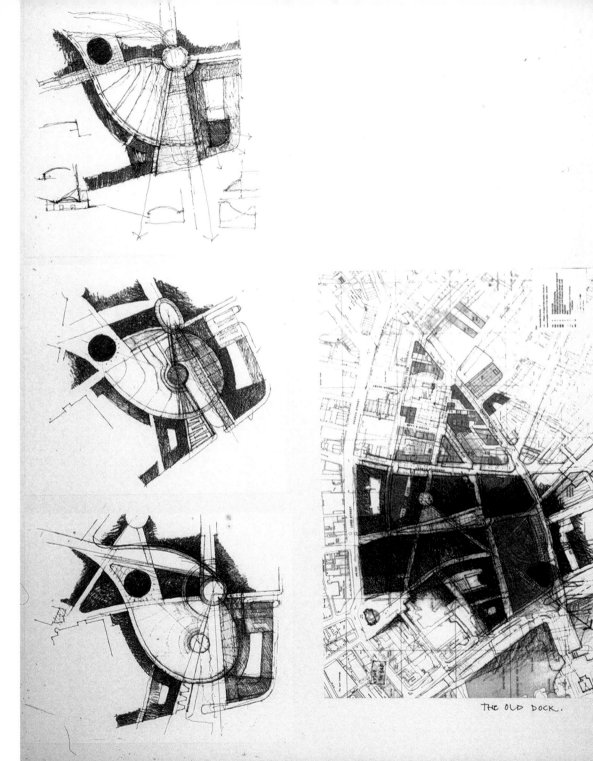

THE OLD DOCK.

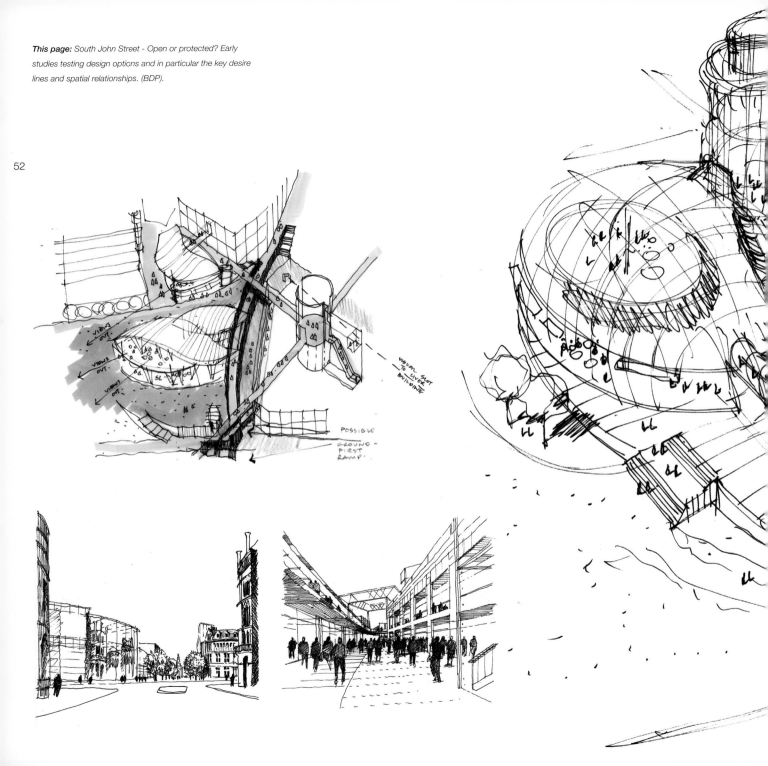

This page: South John Street - Open or protected? Early studies testing design options and in particular the key desire lines and spatial relationships. (BDP).

VIEWS OUT

VIEWS OUT

VIEWS OUT

VISUAL SLOT TO LIVER BUILDING

POSSIBLE GROUND - FIRST RAMP

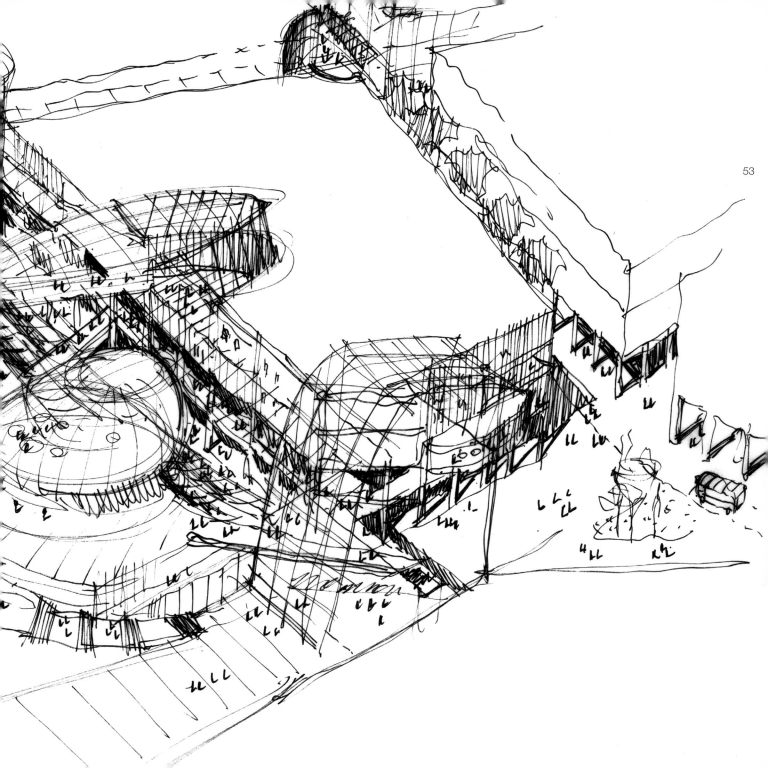

54 **This page and opposite;**
*Emerging character –
development sketches
exploring design options
including the Church Street /
School Lane link. (BDP).*

This page: Top; *The old
Woolworths frontage on
Church Street as a gateway
to the eastern side of the
PSDA. (BDP).*
Bottom; *Massing study for
South John Street and the
anchor stores. (BDP).*

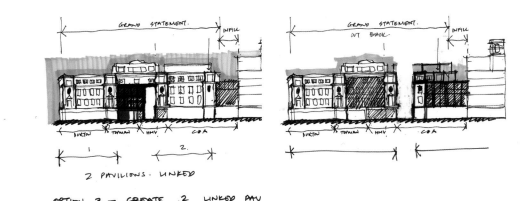

2 PAVILIONS. LINKED

OPTION 3 — CREATE 2 LINKED PAV

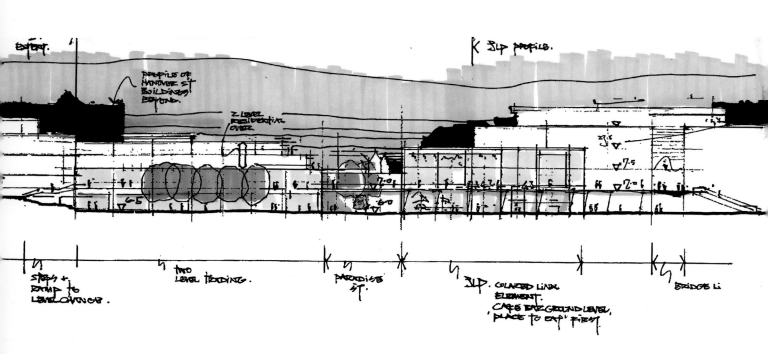

INVITATION TO AXIS

*This page: **Top;** Early thoughts on the linkage through Bluecoat Triangle. **Bottom;** Paradise Street as a pedestrian and tram environment. (BDP).*

Produced in June 2000, this sketch section looking

north through the western side of the project

defines many of the core objectives delivered in the

completed Liverpool One scheme:

- *Undercroft parking between the Strand and Paradise Street*
- *Fully concealed servicing routes*
- *Pavilions in the park*
- *Leisure focus at the head of the park*
- *South John Street as a two level retail destination*
- *A landmark building (site 6) – to the east of Paradise Street as a visual anchor to the vista from the waterfront*
- *The 'discovery axis' – a convenient and direct grade level route between the retail core and the waterfront*

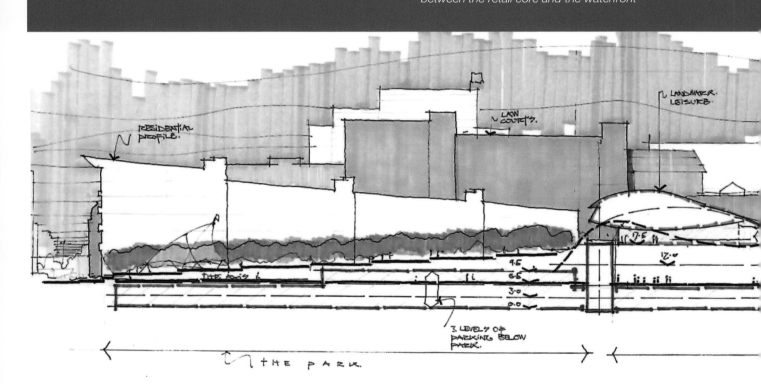

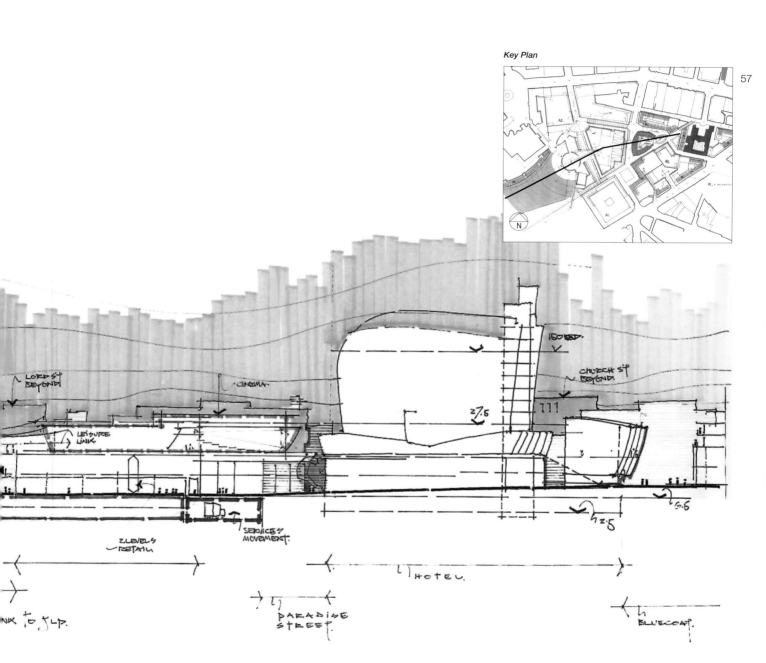

Key Plan

57

LORD S†
BEYOND

CINEMA.

150 BED

CHURCH S†
BEYOND.

LEISURE
LINK

27.5

111

2 LEVELS
RETAIL

SERVICES
MOVEMENT.

23.5

5.5

HOTEL.

LINK TO J.L.P.

PARADISE
STREET.

BLUECOAT.

N

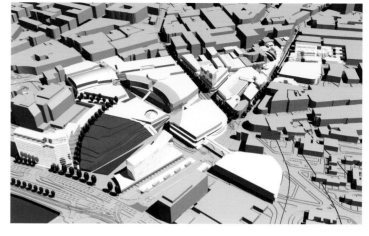

'Buildings in the city'

Developed with Grosvenor as a simple block definition of the emerging masterplan, the 3D computer model proved enormously helpful.

Key landmark buildings including the Anglican Cathedral, Liver Building, Civic Buildings and St John's Tower were surveyed to ensure accurate positioning within the emerging streetscape and vistas.

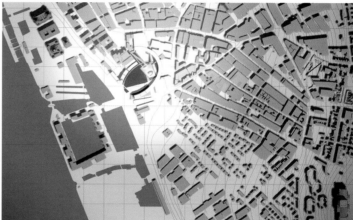

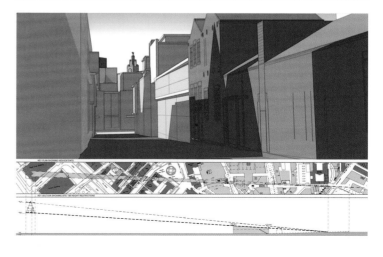

Right: One of several studies capturing the key vistas looking from both within and back into the PSDA site. This study capturing the view down College Lane towards the Liver Building, Bluecoat Chambers to the right. (BDP).

planning
strategy

4

Computer generated image
of finished project (final
image version - Uniform).

liverpool's planning significance

62 Liverpool One's path to completion merits a closer look in terms of the sometimes fairly technical but crucial planning hurdles it had to overcome.

The project started life in 1999, entered the formal planning arena in 2001, and achieved its final discharge of conditions in autumn 2008 in time for Liverpool One's grand opening.

But during this period, notes Terry Davenport, the planning legislation context had moved on. Specifically, the most significant changes were the 2004 Planning and Compulsory Purchase Act, a new list of reserved matters, and new requirements for inclusion in outline planning applications.

Despite these changes, however, Davenport believes the planning approach adopted as part of the Liverpool One scheme has stood the test of time. BDP's strong, overarching masterplan actually included a similar level of information to what would be required to be submitted with outline planning applications today. In fact, the masterplan document could be seen in many ways as a precursor to the current Design and Access Statement requirements.

It is also an approach - that is, having an overarching masterplan for a development site to set the context for future detailed development to evolve - that has set the tone for the next series of town and city centre projects, such as in Sheffield and Bracknell. The masterplans in these cases can now, however, take the form of a Supplementary Planning Document (SPD) or a Design and Access Statement to support an outline planning permission.

The overarching principles employed allowed the plethora of architects designing the individual buildings to work to a common goal. The individual design briefs in the masterplan justified bulk, massing and uses that were acceptable to Liverpool City Council and provided a starting point for the detailed design of the sites moving forward. Although many of the individual sites were submitted as new 'slot-in' planning applications (as the detailed schemes lay outside the outline parameters set in the masterplan) the principle of the development and broad scale remained and allowed the planning applications to be dealt with quickly and without repetition of policy or environmental justification.

The formal planning application process, led throughout by Drivers Jonas, commenced in January 2001 with the submission of a hybrid planning application for the 42 acre site in Liverpool city centre. This planning application followed over two years of extensive consultation with the city council and key stakeholders on the proposals for the Paradise Street Development Area (PSDA which later became Liverpool One).

A 'hybrid' planning application meant that detailed planning permission was being sought for five sites where sufficient detail was needed to assess the developments on the conservation area or listed building. Outline planning permission, with only details of siting and access provided, was sought for the remaining sites.

The hybrid planning application was submitted with extensive supporting information due to the size and complexity of the development site. One of the key documents was the PSDA masterplan produced by BDP. As we have seen, this was a critical document, as it set the scene for the whole development, including the concepts of linkages with the main retail area (MRA) and shopper-flows. The masterplan also included a significant amount of explanation and context, in addition to the floor schedules and indicative scale, massing and height for each site. The January 2001 hybrid application was also supported by a full Environmental Impact Assessment, including a socio-economic chapter and transport assessment.

Revisions were made to the scheme in October 2001 and an updated masterplan was produced and submitted with this

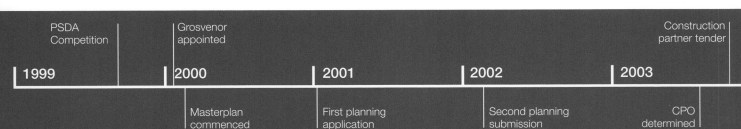

PSDA Competition — 1999

Grosvenor appointed — 2000
Masterplan commenced

First planning application — 2001

Second planning submission — 2002

Construction partner tender

CPO determined — 2003

revised application.

But things were also changing in the background in terms of local legislature. During the consideration of the original planning application, Liverpool City Council was progressing its emerging planning policy framework by updating its Unitary Development Plan (UDP). However, the emerging UDP at the time made no mention of the PSDA scheme. In light of this and the threat of a challenge to the proposals - an objection was received from an alternative scheme in Walton - Liverpool City Council decided to delay the adoption of the UDP, allowing for the planning policy position to be strengthened in support of the Grosvenor scheme and giving more weight to the planning application.

Although this caused a delay, the final adopted UDP provided full support to the PSDA as a solution to enhance the city centre and extend the MRA. The specific policy also confirmed that a comprehensive approach was required to regenerate this part of the city centre. This approach lent weight to the Compulsory Purchase Order (CPO) process and provided a response to objectors who, although supportive of the scheme, felt that it did not require their site to be compulsorily acquired and that they could deliver an element of the overall scheme on their site, whether for retail, residential or hotel use. The UDP was finally adopted and planning permission was granted for the PSDA in December 2002, including a signed Section 106 Agreement.

The CPO inquiry duly followed. But during that process further changes to the scheme were being developed, including alterations to the bus station and tram alignment to incorporate the proposed Merseytram scheme. A new application was required, mainly due to the change in the boundary of the overall development site and amendments to a number of the site boundaries and proposed land uses.

It was at this point that it was felt that further flexibility could be built into the scheme via allowing for a hotel north and hotel south option - either on Site 11 or Site 12, either side of the park. This second hybrid application was submitted, again with full supporting information, to Liverpool City Council in February 2004. Because much of the scheme remained unchanged, the authority was able to determine the application quickly, taking it to committee four months later. The Section 106 Agreement was signed shortly after and planning permission was issued on 9 July 2004.

So, as of July 2004, recalls Davenport, the team had a planning permission, a confirmed CPO and a pressing deadline for a finished development. However, despite five years of work, the development could not commence just yet.

In November 2004 though, all of the final strands - essentially phasing and site-wide strategies - came together. Planning permission had been granted for Sites 10A, 17 and 13D. The development agreement had been signed, funding was in place and an agreement with the anchor stores had been reached. So, in a blaze of publicity, a JCB digger commenced the development with Cllr Mike Storey and the Duke of Westminster taking turns at its controls. The earth had moved.

From this point on, an agreed construction programme was put in place, with milestone dates set for getting the details submitted on all 35 sites to allow construction to commence. Grosvenor had made its decision that it wanted a number of different architects to work on the project, ranging from internationally acclaimed firms to more locally based teams. However, they would all be working to the approved BDP masterplan, which set the framework for the detailed design to be developed. BDP, as the overall masterplanners, continued as the executive architects on the majority of the project.

Start on site — 2005

Bus station & car park open — 2006

West side retail opens — 2008

Eastern side & Park opens

2004 | 2005 | 2006 | 2007 | 2008

Final planning application

64

Grosvenor took the decision following the granting of planning permission in July 2004 that Drivers Jonas would stay involved as planning consultants to liaise with the concept architects as part of detailed design, to co-ordinate and submit all of the future planning submissions, and to act as a single point of contact for Liverpool City Council for all planning matters.

Coordination of so many architects and consultants was clearly going to be a complex matter. So as part of the management of the planning process, regular planning updates and conditions updates were circulated to Grosvenor, its consultants, and Liverpool City Council to keep everyone in the loop. The planning update was submitted fortnightly to over 50 people between November 2004 and December 2008. It provided information on which planning submissions had been submitted and approved in the last two weeks, the current status of the planning submissions awaiting approval, and which planning submissions were being prepared. This planning update formed the basis of the planning discussions at the fortnightly Co-ordination Meetings.

A Conditions Update was also circulated to a similar mailing list on alternative weeks between January 2006 and October 2008. The purpose of this update was to summarise each of the 800 planning conditions across the main July 2004 planning consent and the subsequent 60-plus planning consents. It detailed what information had been submitted and approved in the previous

two weeks and highlighted what information was still outstanding. This document proved invaluable to both Grosvenor and the council in submitting information pursuant to all of the planning conditions before the two phases of Liverpool One opened in 2008. No stone was being left unturned.

Crucially, however, people relationships remained key to the smooth running of the entire process. One of the most important and effective elements of ensuring that the planning process ran smoothly was the good relationship between Grosvenor, Drivers Jonas and the planning officers at Liverpool City Council - particularly with Mike Burchnall, Brian Boardman, Jenny Forshaw and Peter Jones. Both Burchnall and Forshaw were involved from the very beginning of the process when the council went out to tender for the selection of a development partner.

Davenport believes this consistency of personnel and knowledge across Grosvenor, the masterplan team, and Liverpool City Council proved invaluable in helping to deliver robust planning submissions and secure the various planning permissions across the site. 'This excellent relationship between developer and local planning authority is quite refreshing and in stark contrast to some experiences elsewhere in the UK', he says. Both parties sought the same end product - the delivery of a world class city centre for Liverpool - with the project planning team and planning officers speaking on a weekly, if not bi-weekly, basis to ensure that any number of planning submissions at a particular time were moving along well.

The Planning Application

- 42 acres
- 22 sites
- 2.5 million ft² total space
- 1.4 million ft² retail space
- 230,000 ft² leisure space
- 25,000 ft² office space
- 2 hotels
- Over 500 residential units
- Relocated bus interchange
- 3000 parking spaces
- Public park

View of the 1:200 development model looking into the project from above the Albert Dock. (Model by Studioscope).

So, wonders Davenport, what if - in theory - the team was to start the planning process all over again? What lessons have been learned?

Davenport believes BDP's experiences over the nine-year life of Liverpool One project have revealed that within any new planning process there are a number of key aspects required. The first is a strong masterplan. The second would be a parameter plan-based approach within that masterplan to allow flexibility for design development, possibly providing a footprint area, rather than precise boundary. On reflection, Davenport believes this might have reduced the number of sites having to be submitted as new 'slot-in' planning applications as part of the PSDA. Thirdly, satisfying the minimum information for outline applications at the time was a major consideration. Going forward under current planning requirements, this is still very much the case, with a thorough and robust masterplan key to underpinning the outline process. Flexibility, as we have seen, was also a major component, and in terms of planning this was essentially including as much flexibility with regard to conditions as possible. This could allow changes in the design of buildings to be dealt with via conditions rather than, in the worst cases, the need for a new planning consent. Finally, and fundamentally, there was the human factor that stitches all this together – the forging of a good relationship with the local planning authority at all levels, each with a single common goal emphasised in its very name: Liverpool One.

This page: Top; A 'proposal' for a city airport at the Pier Head. The Evening Express, 1934. (LCC).
Bottom left; Towers and terraces overlooking the

Strand and Paradise Street and a new six and a half acre park. Paradise Street Plan, 1965. (LCC).
Bottom right; Sketch of proposed Civic Centre in

South Castle Street area 1965, with the Victoria Monument to the right. (LCC).

Opposite page: Top; Shankland's vision with the Three Graces just visible in the top right corner. Parallels with PSDA are evident. 1965. (LCC).

Bottom left; Sketch of proposed Civic Centre in South Castle Street area. 1965. (LCC).
Top right; Graphic illustration of the Paradise Street plan.

1965. (Copy LCC).
Bottom right; Sketch proposal for a covered arcade along Bold Street. 1965. (LCC).

66

Post War Vision

Graeme Shankland was a leading British post-war architect.

The Liverpool City Centre Plan (1965) was a city wide strategy produced by the city planning department in parallel with Graeme Shankland (Shankland Cox Associates). The plan was to provide a progressive solution for reshaping the city's central area and a template for control of development, guidance on standards, public awareness and consultation of planning the city centre.

It was to be a brave, visionary design led plan for one of the country's foremost cities; a plan that would be used to provide a positive and inspirational model for others to follow. Indeed it is revealing to find that some of the recommendations and strategies from the plan include;

- Encouraging a return to city centre living
- Promoting cultural developments
- Permeability to the riverside
- Increasing pedestrianisation
- Creating more public space

Some 45 years later, elements of that vision have finally been delivered.

Masterplan drawing depicting the
22 individual sites. The buildings
in the darker grey were submitted
as detailed applications with the
remainder of the sites submitted
as outline under the hybrid
application. (BDP).

68

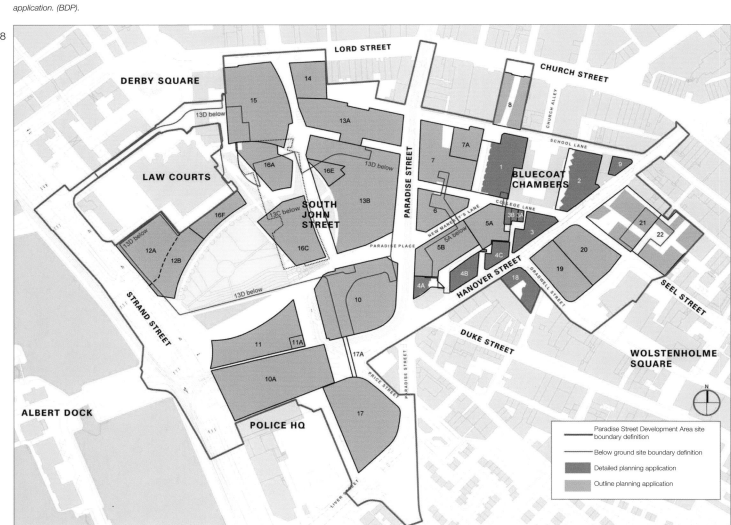

	A	Anchor Units
	B	Single-level Unit Shopping
	C	Multi-level Unit Shopping (Ground & Upper level)
	D	Grade Level Unit Shopping (Single Level)
	E	Upper Level Unit Shopping (Single Level)
	F	Residential
	G	MSU
	H	Ancillary/Upper Level Occupancy/Office
	L	Leisure Element
	M	Hotel
	N	Landscaped Space
	P	Speciality Retail Market / Upper and High Level
	Q	Central Facilities
		Park
		Car Park
		Anchor Store Loading Dock / Goods Handling

The key masterplan layouts submitted with the final planning application. The blue tones indicate different types of retail activity with a wide range of uses integrated. (BDP).

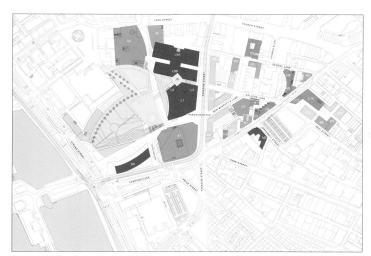

Plan at Grade Level

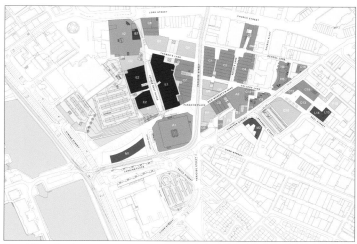

Plan at Upper Level

Plan at High Level

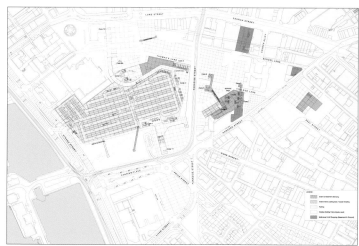

Plan at Upper Basement Level

concept
designs

5

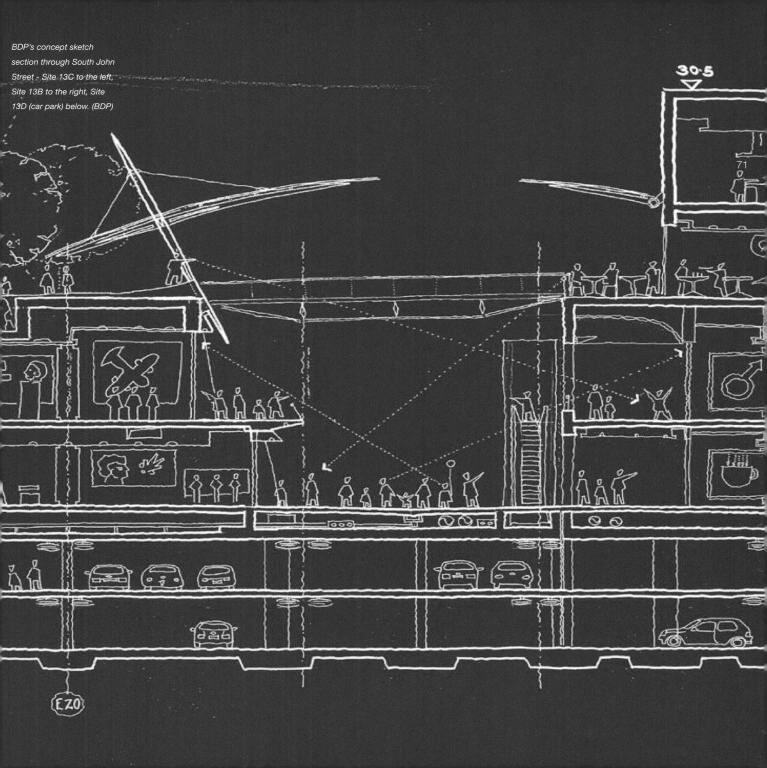

BDP's concept sketch
section through South John
Street - Site 13C to the left,
Site 13B to the right, Site
13D (car park) below. (BDP)

concept response

The Liverpool One project is extraordinary in the way it has harnessed creativity from a number of separate sources, forging a new and sizeable piece of city in what many observers believe is an exemplary - albeit hugely complex - process. Happily, the whole is proving to be even greater than the considerable sum of its parts.

Essentially, as we have seen, a robust masterplan was created by BDP which allowed it and other architects to design individual buildings, coming together for workshop sessions and extensive consultation with key stakeholders such as CABE and English Heritage along the way. As defined by the hybrid masterplan approach, the majority of the buildings went to outline planning; the sites around the listed Bluecoat Chambers in the Ropewalks area took a different approach, with the architects responsible for the individual buildings there, including BDP, taking their schemes to detailed design. But although over 20 different architects have contributed to the overall project, Liverpool One avoids being an 'architectural zoo'. Rather, the methods adopted have fostered creativity and coordinated different 'voices' - just as any other urban setting has accrued over the years.

Howarth Tompkins, for example, was brought on board to design two buildings on three sites - formally known as sites 7, 3, 3A and B. Site 7 fronts onto Paradise Street and occupies the end of an urban block, which the practice responded to with a large blue-brick building of four storeys of residential above two of retail, featuring a blue metallic grid. A slab block opens up into a courtyard along a side street, connecting with the back of an arcade which runs down Peter's Lane. The architect's other building is a much smaller affair - three storeys on Hanover Street which, as it turns the corner down College Lane, sets back with a series of roof-like terraces which respect the scale of Bluecoat Chambers.

Howarth Tompkins was on the project from the very early days. Practice partner Graham Howarth recalls the process of selection as being a very informal series of interviews where developer Grosvenor looked at architects who could show experience of working in dense urban contexts. 'There was a lot of very strong contextual work that was needed in terms of fitting in with the scale and the grain of the existing architecture', he says. From then on it was a case of Grosvenor and BDP feeling which practice would be most suited to which site. Page and Park was selected to design the BBC Radio building, again abutting the Bluecoat building, which had a very specific, technical end user requirement. Brock Carmichael worked to its strengths with a residential conversion and BDP developed the adjacent hotel design. Howarth Tompkins wrote to Grosvenor's Rod Holmes to say that, actually, it quite fancied the look of Site 3. Following an initial period with Allford Hall Monaghan Morris, Jeremy Dixon came in to work on Site 1, designing an arcade that was not part of the masterplan at the time. 'That again was part of the way of different architects being able to bring different things to the mix', says Howarth. 'It was quite an enlightened way of working'.

Design workshops followed. Initially, these were held In BDP's Liverpool office prior to Grosvenor acquiring its Lord Street base. 'They were with Terry Davenport and Rod Holmes, who are very hands-on', says Howarth. 'We just bounced ideas around and we had a series of workshops with all the architects who were working opposite us, particularly Page \ Park, because they were immediately opposite us on the street. We worked on a collective model together so we'd bring our building, they'd bring their building, and we'd put them in a sort of common site plan and look at how the conversations between the buildings might work. That led to Page \ Park's building - they introduced a curve like an arc in the back of the building.' The scheme, which houses the BBC and the Religious Society of Friends, steps down to the Bluecoat Chambers, with the curve forming an echo of the Bluecoat building itself. David Page takes up the story: 'Bluecoat is a diminutive two-and-a-half storey building surrounded by big existing buildings and potentially even bigger new neighbours. It was all about a kind of homage.'

Page \ Park worked with The Friends and the BBC as two separate components, observing in the Bluecoat's geometry the bow-windowed curve of the courtyard and College Lane, whose geometry is set out by the centre point of the courtyard on the other side. 'So it was kind of like one courtyard sets up another courtyard and its geometry. Likewise, we then introduced a concave curve to our courtyard terrace, generated from the centre point of the dome of the Bluecoat building.'

Page describes his building as having two distinct characters - an open, non-defensive aspect for the BBC which led the architect to explore the terrace form, like a conservatory wrapping round onto Hanover Street, merged with the Friends' more defensive, quieter view, rendering the terraces more solid and brick-like as they extend towards the Friends' building. The BBC element includes three studios, an open theatre and ground floor shop. On the front of the Bluecoat building is an evocation of the wing of a phoenix, and that is how Page conceived the building - as a feathered wing or protective, nurturing wrapping around the setting of the Bluecoat.

These are just two examples of the many practices involved in the site. Wilkinson Eyre designed the bus interchange as one of the first schemes to be built at Liverpool One and an elegant pedestrian bridge to the car park, plus, incidentally, the Arena project on the waterfront, while Pelli Clarke Pelli Architects had design input into the park and designed the 22-storey mixed use tower building on the waterfront. Besides BDP, there were many others to coordinate - Ainsley Gomman, which designed the Friends' Meeting House (fit out), Allies and Morrison; Austin: Smith-Lord, BDP's own offices in Glasgow, Liverpool and London, CZWG, FAT, Glenn Howells, Greig & Stephenson, Gross Max, which designed the water feature, Groupe 6, Hawkins Brown, Marks Barfield, Michael Squire & Partners/Aedas, Stephenson Bell, Owen Ellis Partnership and Studio Three. All in all, it was a major team effort.

Both Page and Howarth commend the masterplan process and the sense that Liverpool was - and is - a place on the move. 'There was a palpable sense that the city was going to change dramatically with this development, and everybody wanted to really make sure that it got off on the right foot', remembers Howarth. 'It was almost open book working that Grosvenor instigated, particularly with Rod. He's an amazing catalyst in all of this. He puts in a lot of energy and has a really good way of communicating the way that the design process works.'

Effective communication with community groups and stakeholders was also a major part of this process, with locals who were going to be immediately affected by some of the Ropewalks works, such as the Quakers. The architects also received a lot of feedback from planners. 'It was very noticeable that design officers were available to talk to us about the design - they were very keen to make sure that they facilitated the process.'

Plenary sessions with the design team, masterplan team, various site architects and all the interested parties such as English Heritage, design panel advisors and planning officers contributed to a 'pro-active' and 'dynamic' process, added Howarth. 'It was really just a case of realising that the scheme was important - it was going to kick-start a lot of regeneration, and I think Grosvenor and BDP did have this vision. They had an understanding of the scale of it. I think they were very fresh in terms of their approach.'

Page agrees. 'I think BDP has played a remarkable role', he says. 'Working with Terry Davenport and his colleagues was a very open, creative process that's the sort of thing you should do on any ideas on any urban site.'

For many, this approach is a new but effective way of building large chunks of city - a similar story to that at Brindley Place in Birmingham and with developer Argent at the King's Cross development to come. But for Page this was remarkable in terms of its scale and the 'amazing' way such a 'brave' decision was carried out. 'It is very impressive, bringing all these different designers together', he says. 'I think they were all motivated by this sense of creating a distinctive place.'

And for some, this process replaces a void left by the traditional role of the planner as they become more overworked. 'For a city centre scheme of this sort of size it's a fantastic way of working because it means that you get the diversity but you also get the overview and the vision of the masterplanners and client', says Howarth.

The process also meant that where calm buildings were required, appropriate architects were selected, while design competitions were held for the larger, more prominent buildings - such as the department stores.

John McAslan was selected to design the John Lewis building and Allies and Morrison for site 13B, the largest block in the Paradise Street project. Bordering four streets at ground level - Paradise Street, Paradise Place, South John Street and Thomas's Lane, it is surrounded by other new buildings including the two anchor stores - John Lewis and Debenhams - and a multi-screen cinema. The building contains 45 retail units and 16 cafes / bars / restaurants, as well as the entrance to the multi-screen cinema, all linking through to the park and retail 'street' below and featuring that distinctive 'zig-zag' stair. Glenn Howells competed in, and won, a competition to design a scheme for the island Site 6.

Ultimately, the concept designs come together to form a unified whole, enhanced by

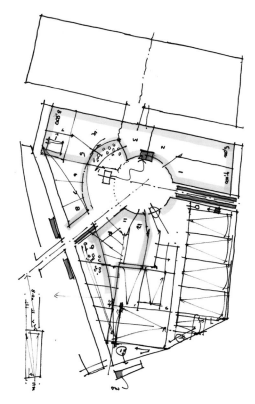

One of many sketch plans testing design options to inform the buildings' briefs - Site 13B. (BDP).

74 BDP's high quality public realm and lighting design throughout. Howarth believes that in the Bluecoat triangle, where his practice completed his buildings, there are very different conditions to those in play on the other side of Paradise Street, with its larger-scale retail buildings. But there is a very strong transition between the two. Page agrees, but does not see a problem in having different characters anyway - great cities have changes in character across their urban fabric, and his firm's BBC building is a case in point where it has been modified between different scales. Moreover, the project focused on a number of different quarters - informal Hanover Street, busy, prime shopping Peter's Lane, city boulevard-like Paradise Street, vibrant South John Street and the varied Pool and park, each with its own different character and ambience. 'I think the ability to embrace a range of concepts for different areas of the city within one development is an astonishing act of imagination', says Page.

So what of Liverpool One as a whole? How has the masterplan performed? For Howarth it has been 'hugely successful'. 'It will be a fantastic honey-pot for the whole area', he says. Where there was once a sea of cheap 60s hotels and other sundry buildings, the new landscape is one of a regenerated area stitched into the urban fabric, amongst an array of fine existing buildings.

What has been built is remarkably faithful to the original masterplan visuals, with vistas revealing views of the Liver Building and the impressive diversity of architecture from the corner of Hanover Street looking down College Lane.

For Page the only mystery is why Liverpool did not quite embrace the project as an integral part of its year of culture celebrations. 'It's really a model of performance and I actually see this is about the art of city building', he says. 'It is a story that should be told of the true legacy of the European City of Culture - which is not the museums and stuff like that but this whole, decent city we have built.'

The following pages capture a variety of concept images from across the project's 22 sites. The emerging designs were reviewed at the weekly workshops held over a 4-year period. These were led by Grosvenor and the masterplan team and attended by a wide cross section of people from the city, the planning team, the construction team, lighting and landscape teams and key consultees as appropriate. Regular wider workshops were also arranged to engage a number of the concept teams together and coordinate specific inter site relationships.

BDPs masterplan role on Liverpool One extended well beyond the normal remit. The brief for each site was comprehensively tested, particularly for the buildings surrounding the park, where design and technical interfaces were complex.

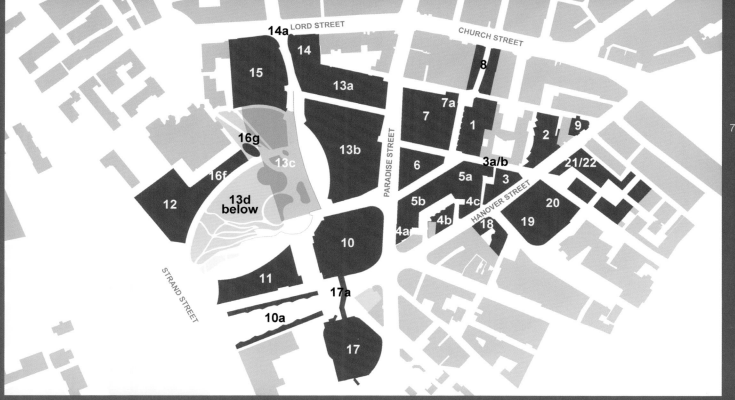

75

The following pages capture a variety of concept images from across the project's 22 sites. The emerging designs were reviewed at the weekly workshops held over a four year period. These were led by Grosvenor and the masterplan team and attended by a wide cross section of people from the city, the planning team, the construction team, lighting and landscape teams and key consultees as appropriate. Regular wider workshops were also arranged to engage a number of the concept teams together and coordinate specific inter site relationships.

Site 1
Architect: Dixon Jones

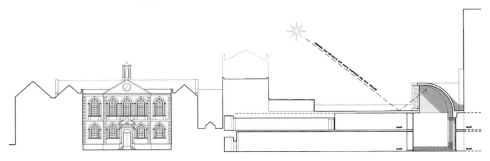

This page: Site 1; This is a building that sets the scale and character of Peter's Lane and forms a public space at each end. It is not a high building due to its relationship with the Bluecoat Chambers. Its visual interest is in the subtlety of its form and detailing and through the manner in which the rhythm of the double height shop front is achieved. The architect for this site has responded to the brief by creating an arcade along Peter's Lane that ties together sites 7, 7a and 1 and is asymmetrical in section to deflect light down into the shopping environment.

Opposite page: Site 2; Site 2 is located between School Lane and Hanover Street adjacent to Abney Buildings. The building reconciles the differences of scale between the relatively low Bluecoat Chambers and the tall Abney Buildings and with a new connecting space complements the fine grain and atmosphere that currently exists. The architect created a semi-circular form focusing on the Bluecoat Chambers with the resulting building stepping back from the listed building on the west. The site 2 building forms a strong edge to Hanover Street on the east and brings the scale of the street down from the Abney Buildings.

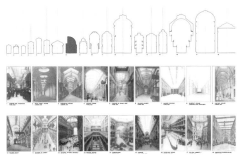

Site 2
Architect: Page \ Park

2

Site 3 & 3a/b
Architect: Haworth Tompkins

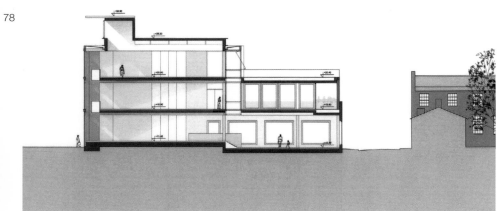

Site 3 & 3a/b; *Located on the corner of College Lane/Hanover Street, the site presents a prominent corner, visible especially from the north and east.*

There is scope to emphasise this through the continuation of scale of the adjacent Stanley Buildings, although the massing on College Lane needs to respect the single storey rear of the Bluecoat Chambers and the height and width of the two listed Merchants' Warehouses on College Lane. The site is extended to the west of these warehouses to further enable sensitive treatments in this area. The architect has responded to these issues and, in addition, has created a pedestrian link running from College Lane to Hanover Street, revealing the rear of the listed warehouses. This forms a continuation of the new pedestrian linkage created on site 2.

3/3ab

SITE 3   SITE 3A   SITE 3B

PASSAGEWAY

Site 4a, b & c
Architect: Brock Carmichael Architects

Site 4a, b & c; Through the retention of the existing buildings and sensitive new infill proposals, the continuity of scale of buildings in Hanover Street is maintained and a sympathetic refurbishment of the buildings on Paradise Street achieved. The architect's response to these sites has been considered and in keeping with the context of the development, including well mannered facades along Hanover Street and carefully designed side elevations.

Site 5b
Architect: Stephenson Bell

Site 5b; *This building anchors New Manesty's Lane and turns the corner onto Paradise Street thus linking two different scales – the intimacy of warehouse vernacular and the expanse of boulevard space. The striking glass lantern responds to the views and vistas informing the site with the architect making strong reference to the link with Thomas Steers Way and the Albert Dock beyond.*

5b

Site 6
Architect: Glenn Howells Architects

Site 6; *A tall landmark building between Paradise Street, New Manesty's Lane and College Lane in the very heart of Liverpool One. Physically constrained by these streets the building responds by creating a massing hierarchy that delivers the main tower facing Paradise Street and focusing on the visual axis to the waterfront.*

The building comprises a three level podium of retail accommodation topped by a ten level residential tower. A rooftop courtyard and garden space provides some relief and animation at podium level above retail accommodation.

Site 7 & 7a
Architect: Haworth Tompkins with Brock Carmichael Architects

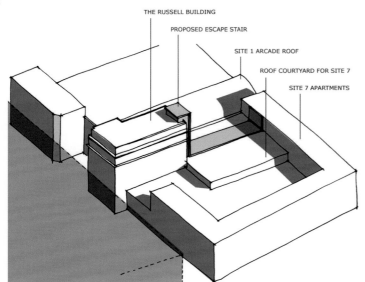

THE RUSSELL BUILDING

PROPOSED ESCAPE STAIR

SITE 1 ARCADE ROOF

ROOF COURTYARD FOR SITE 7

SITE 7 APARTMENTS

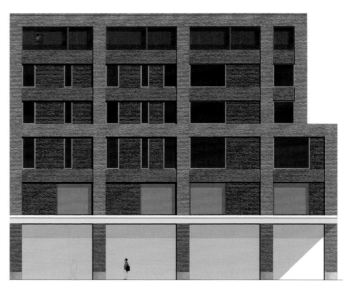

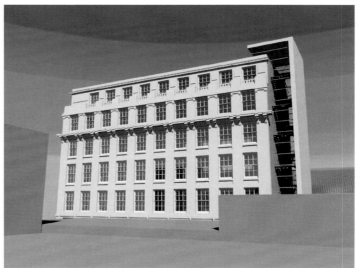

Site 8
Architect: Greig & Stephenson

Site 8 pavilion
Architect: FAT

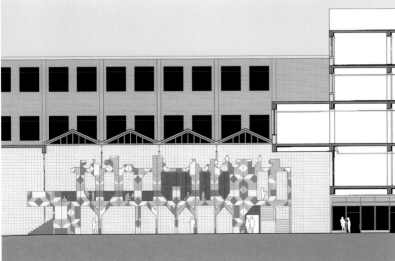

Opposite page: Site 7 & 7a; *A large island block between Paradise Street and College Lane also fronting Peter's Lane and School Lane with the existing Russell Building (Site 7a).*

With a long elevation onto Paradise Street, the architect has reduced the building scale by introducing a rhythm of structure and fenestration expressed through the brickwork.

A mixed use residential and retail building, the retail units front onto Paradise Street with access from College Lane to four residential levels plus a creche facility above. The roof of the retail elements forms a private terrace for use by the residents.

This page: Site 8; *Conversion of an existing pair of large retail stores fronting Church Street into one destination store and the creation of a double height arcade with shop units breaking through to Peter's Lane at the rear.*

The new connection, sympathetic to the strong symmetry of the Church Street façade, provides key permeability into Liverpool One and reinforces the public square at the entrance to Peter's Lane Arcade. The unusual section of the original building has been used to capture an excellent quality of daylight with 'Keys Court'.

Site 8 pavilion;
The master plan brief called for a pavilion to be created within the new arcade that must evoke a sense of place, possibly reflecting the period of the existing, rejuvenated host building around it; or a memorable piece of contemporary design. The architects FAT (Fashion Architecture Taste) responded with a strong design for a colourful and distinctive pavilion that frames one side of the arcade and creates a series of spaces for retailers and the public alike.

Site 9
Architect: CZWG Architects

Site 9; *This is one of the first Liverpool One buildings to be delivered and perhaps the building that has courted most debate. Referred to as the Bling Bling building, the architect responded pragmatically to difficult site constraints although with obvious design intent and flair.*

Situated on the corner of School Lane and Hanover Street, it is an important approach to the north eastern corner of Liverpool One. An infill corner site, the architect had to respect existing rights of light from adjacent buildings and successfully reconstruct the urban fabric.

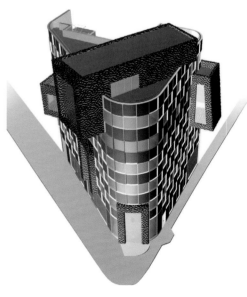

Site 10
Architect: John McAslan + Partners

Top: Site 10;

One of two anchor stores within PSDA, this building is
located on the corner of Canning Place and Paradise Street.
The building responds to its pivotal position with important
frontages on all four sides. The form and massing addresses
the Ropewalks and Hanover Street Quarter to the south east,
Paradise Street, Canning Place and the transport interchange
to the west and the grand setting of the park to the north.
The grid of the building is aligned with the edge of the old
Canning Dock and the western elevation cantilevers out to add
protection. The elipse of the park slices through the corner
of the building and is expressed on the roof in the form of a
canopy. The roof is also set back to frame views across to the
Cathedral from Chavasse Park.

(For Site 10a see illustration on page 95, Wilkinson Eyre)

Site 11
Architect: Squire and Partners

Site 11; On the corner of Strand Street and Canning Place a substantial landmark building of ten storeys forming part of the elliptical composition of the park and the southern half of a framed entrance to the park from the west. The profile steps down towards the park offering continuous active frontage along Thomas Steers Way. The building has spectacular views in all directions, but particularly to the west and north. The building offers some weather protection on its north side in the form of a colonnade.

Site 12
Architect: Pelli Clarke Pelli Architects

Site 12; *Situated on the north west corner of Chavasse Park along Strand Street, a seventeen storey building providing a significant landmark onto the waterfront.*

The striking building form with its canted prow responds directly to both the Strand and Chavasse Park. Along the Strand it imposes a scale synonymous with the waterfront and to Chavasse Park, its geometry reflects a curve that is part of the grand ellipse within the masterplan.

It also steps down to the east merging with the landform within Chavasse Park and ultimately the reduced scale of South John Street.

A car park structure is incorporated beneath and to the rear of the building. Modern apartments are created with balconies helping to create a safe environment by overlooking the park.

Site 13a
Architect: BDP

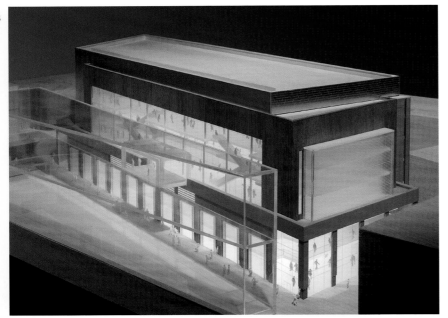

Site 13a; *The large scale form of the cinema building is conceived as a series of interlocking blocks composed of different materials.*

The retail base of the building is articulated in terracotta planks, with extruded terracotta corner details to the expressed columns and pilasters. Triple height shopfronts open onto Paradise Street and South John Street. Contextually there are a number of fine terracotta buildings in the city, including No. 12 Hanover Street, by Edmund Kirby, which forms a visual stop to the south end of Paradise Street.

The cinema above comprises two simple interlocking volumes of copper and stainless steel. The reflective steel is reminiscent of the shimmer of light on the Mersey, and softens the silhouette of the building when viewed from the new Chavasse Park and Albert Dock. The glazed circulation atrium opens up the cinema to passers by and offers great views of the city.

The upper level Sky Bar provides a dramatic vista of the city roofscape, highlighting views to the Anglican Cathedral, the Liver Building and the Mersey.

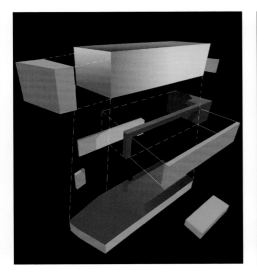

Site 13b
Architect: Allies and Morrison

Site 13b; *Of all the city blocks, this one is a landmark building of considerable scale. It is significant and expressive as it underpins and aligns the overall street character with the masterplan objectives. This urban block occupies not only the heart of the Liverpool One scheme but also provides the fundamental link between the east and west sides of Liverpool One as defined by Paradise Street.*

The building's elevation along Paradise Street and indeed Paradise Place extends the formal scale and influence of the Church Street/Lord Street facades.

Along the western side of the block, the elevation creates a formal two level colonnade providing a protected route to the street. The south west corner of the restaurant terrace is cut away to reveal the critical vista from the head of Chavasse Park to the Anglican Cathedral.

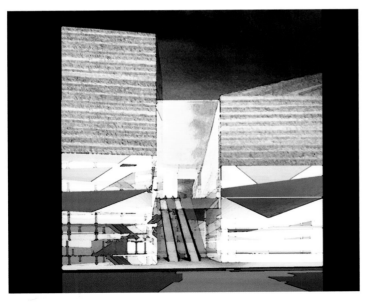

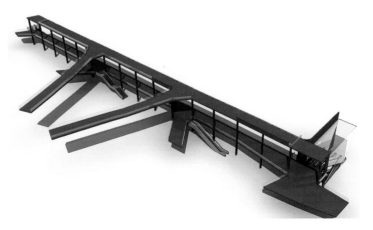

Site 13c
Architect: BDP

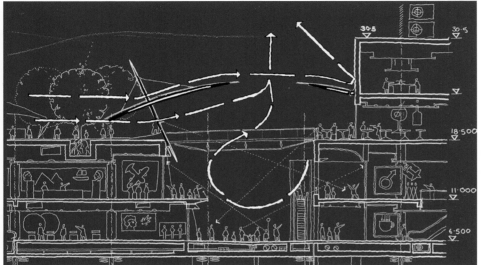

Site 13c; *The foundations to this building have been cut into the red sandstone rock that formed the original rock outcrop on which Liverpool castle was built over 800 years ago.*

Elements of the building have been cut from this material and are used in a traditional though modern way with the 'red wall' forming the main part of the façade at grade level manifesting itself at each end of the building as stone 'bookends' to South John Street.'

Its main façade forms the western side of South John Street and accommodates two separate levels of shopping. It provides the backdrop to a key pedestrian circulation route connecting Lord Street at one end and Paradise Place at the other. This circulation works on two levels and naturally exploits differences in level across the site to provide a space in which to promenade both within the street and on upper terraces. Its roof is Chavasse Park, including trees, planting, soils and grass which gradually reduces in height to meet The Strand on its western side.

Behind and beneath it lies the subterranean multi-storey car park and, crucially, a vast array of mechanical and electrical services equipment (13d site).

Its southern side, facing the Hilton Hotel, accommodates Sugar House Steps and the bespoke terraces which accommodate the various cafés and restaurants.

At the upper level, bridges link to the various shops and restaurants on the opposite site 13b in a dynamic way. Within the theatre of this street there are clear dramatic views that visually connect each level and evoke an awareness of the presence of the park above. The canopy forms a sheltered loggia affording views both deep into the scheme and out to the Wirral across the Albert Dock.

Site 14
Architect: BDP

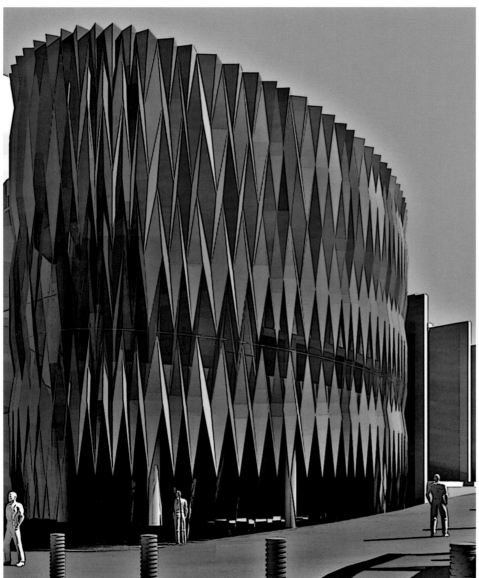

Site 14; *Positioned opposite Debenhams, again with BDP as architect and including a Marks Barfield designed façade to the South John Street corner, the appearance of this building continues the same sympathetic scale and provides the mechanism to turn the corner from South John Street onto Lord Street. The differences in rhythm and proportion between the two streets are absorbed within the form of the building. Together with the eye catching facade the building visually anchors the corner providing the gateway to Liverpool One from Lord Street and the adjacent business district.*

14

Site 15
Architect: Groupe 6 with BDP

Site 15; *Designed by Groupe 6, BDP's French associate, Site 15 accommodates the new Debenhams store and as a building performs several important roles; In urban terms, it is fundamentally a landmark element of the scheme being visible outside Liverpool One from the existing city centre and anchoring a key corner of the site at the junction of Lord Street and South John Street. For the pedestrian, the building provides both visual and movement links between the park and various street levels, particularly South John Street, offering welcome familiarity and orientation for the public/consumer.*

Groupe 6 has responded architecturally by creating a bold and animated building. The mass of this very large building is not overpowering and has been carefully masked by designing the elevations with a scale and presence compatible with existing public buildings and surrounding streetscape.

15

Site 16f
Architect: BDP

Site 16f; *Sitting adjacent to the Law Courts, this BDP design* 93
ensures a clarity of form which both reinforces the edge and
extends the geometry of the park.

This building is more of a perimeter block rather than pavilion
and, adjacent to site 16g, it's curved form is a substantial
counterpoint to its neighbour's distinctive folds. The design
successfully responds to the park and the masterplan geometry
helping to transform the architectural scale to the dominant site
12 tower.

Its composition ensures key vistas out to the docks and
the park are preserved. Technically, it also provides vital
infrastructure to the park, acting to conceal both the ventilation
intake and exhaust from the 2000 car parking spaces below.

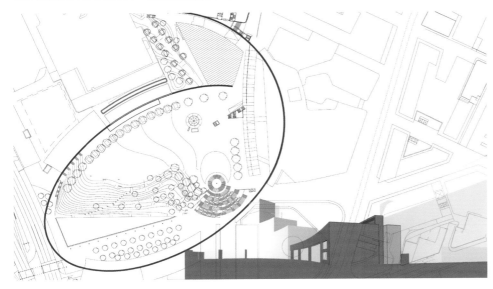

Site 16g
Architect: Studio Three

94

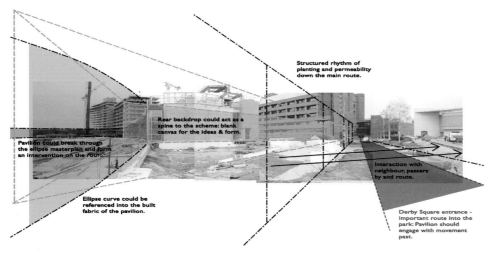

Site 16g; *Located along the path leading from Derby Square into Chavasse Park and overlooked by both the Law Courts and the Debenhams building, this small but jewel-like building typifies the concept of 'pavilion in the park'.*

Designed by Studio Three Architects the distinctive and dynamic architecture responds to a very prescriptive brief that includes enhancing views into the park, across to adjacent buildings and to the wider cityscape. The subtle combination of internal and external space works well to create a place of familiarity, even intimacy.

Structured rhythm of planting and permeability down the main route.

Rear backdrop could act as a spine to the scheme: blank canvas for the ideas & form.

Pavilion could break through the ellipse masterplan and form an intervention on the route.

Ellipse curve could be referenced into the built fabric of the pavilion.

Interaction with neighbour, passers by and route.

Derby Square entrance - important route into the park: Pavilion should engage with movement past.

Sites 17 / 17a / 10a
Architect: Wilkinson Eyre.Architects

Site 17. (left): *The new Liver Street car park, including a taxi rank and bus layover, between Canning Place, Park Lane and Price Street not only provides excellent facilities right in the heart of the city centre, but is an important and imposing building marking a southern gateway to Liverpool One. Architect Wilkinson Eyre has created a successful and striking design which responds to several important approaches, most significantly the north west corner facing the park and the adjacent bus station.*

Site 17a. (bottom right): *This remarkable single span bridge links the car park with the 2nd floor of John Lewis. A sense of drama unfolds (literally) on crossing, as the bridge reveals stunning views to both the waterfront and the city skyline.*

Site 10a - Bus interchange. (bottom left): *Within Canning Place between site 11 and the existing Police Headquarters. Twin 5 bay bus stands to the north and south of the space define the vehicular movement and provide enclosed passenger protection. They form simple uncluttered linear forms reinforcing the geometry of the space and, in particular, its relationship to site 11. Space for a future tram system is accommodated.*

Site 18
Architect: Leach Rhodes Walker

96 **Site 18;** *This building will restore the continuity of the Hanover Street frontage and provide a complementary scale to the adjacent Gostins building. The scale of the building reduces along the Gradwell Street frontage. The corner of Hanover Street and Gradwell Street to be emphasised, possibly with the location of the building entrance and vertical circulation. The brief for this building recognises the flanking wall of Gostins and envisages a courtyard space providing a dynamic atrium for the hotel.*

To the rear at Campbell Street the scale is further influenced by Gostins and an adjacent warehouse structure in Gradwell Street itself. This side is the point for servicing into the rear of the hotel. The materiality of the building is very much of the Hanover Street quarter with the influence of the warmer brick palette being appropriate to its setting.

Site 19/20
Architect: Austin-Smith:Lord

Site 19/20; *The combination of a multi-storey car - and retail destination has been thoughtfully delivered by Austin-Smith:Lord in this pragmatic approach to a large urban block.*

Located along Hanover Street and within the Duke Street Conservation Area, this building restores the large building scale of the street but also reduces its elevational treatment by a series of smaller distinct architectural elements and treatments including retail frontage to the ground floor of Hanover Street and School Lane.

the park

6

Looking onto the World Heritage setting - An evening view along Thomas Steers Way towards the Albert Dock with the impressive Sugar House steps in the foreground. This dramatically captures the relationship between the city's waterfront heritage and the Liverpool One development. The line of the fountain marks the northern edge of the Old Dock.

the park

The park is the green heart of Liverpool One, serving as a central focus in which people can mix and gather, eat and drink, or simply orientate themselves along key sightlines down to the river or into other parts of the site or city. As such a crucial node, therefore, it was critical to get the feel of this space just right.

An understanding of the park's history and context is important in establishing its significance. Davenport sets the scene: 'Liverpool is blessed with many outstanding parks, providing a necklace of green public space encircling its suburbs. But within the city centre itself, due to the sheer intensity of the maritime-led expansion, few exist. Apart from Chavasse Park, only the pier head and St George's Gardens in the heart of the city provide green open space, and both are quite formal and generally underused."

Chavasse Park, as emphasised by the dramatic wartime images, emerged following the bombing and, although simply grassed and ill-defined, it became an important asset to the city. In addition, the naming of the park - after Noel Godfrey Chavasse, one of only three people to be awarded the Victoria Cross twice - gave it even greater significance.

'As the BDP team developed the initial competition proposals, the park in its pivotal location evolved as a natural heartspace not just for the project but for the city centre', says Davenport. 'We had many workshops in the early stages, not least with Mike Storey, who was always quizzing us on the status of the park and its relative size - to the nearest square metre - compared to the post-war Chavasse Park. Although the new masterplan area was broadly compatible, it was difficult at the time to illustrate the sheer quality of the space that was emerging."

Grosvenor director Rod Holmes relates how the Pelli Clarke Pelli (PCP) team had stood out at various presentations with its early thoughts on how the site as a whole could develop. Looking back, he is particularly keen on the ellipse form the team devised as a viable shape for the park with which to draw out the potential in the rest of the area. That was Pelli's resolution to the problem of a number of urban grids meeting at this kink in the alignment of the Mersey. 'It does seem to work very well, and people feel very comfortable in it', Holmes says.

Urban design consultant Trevor Skempton also heaps praise on elements of the park, such as the semi-circular staircase and Sugar House Steps, which he believes help it form an ensemble. It is also a testament, he believes, to the sort of scale of project Pelli is used to working at. 'It has a confidence that gives that central part of the scheme a little bit of credibility', he says.

But before the plaudits continue it is perhaps worthwhile looking back on the genesis of the park and surrounding landscape features to acknowledge the pivotal role it plays in the whole Liverpool One development, and how that emerged.

PCP's ideas ultimately won out as the most analytical and extensive of the three competing teams. And this was what led to the practice winning through to receive a commission to work on the Site 12 building and the park.

Bill Butler of Pelli Clarke Pelli takes up the story: 'The initial BDP masterplan for that edge of Chavasse Park had very good, strong underpinning in terms of connections'. In particular, Butler lists South John Street as it descended south, the concave and straight side, and the two-level shopping street that worked well in terms of accessibility and permeability back into the city. 'The 'Discovery Axis' as it extended east-west towards the Albert Dock was also in place and was also a very good, strong idea about how to connect the city out to the river's edge', says Butler. The edges were being defined by buildings along Paradise Street, alongside the concept of two anchor retail stores either end of South John Street - Debenhams to the north and then John Lewis to the south.

In those early iterations of the masterplan, on the southern edge of the park, says Butler, was one extremely large building - a combination of retail anchor and, adjacent to it at the lower and upper level, the bus terminal. An elliptical hotel sat on the Strand, while at the head of the park at its upper level was a concave building that had the Winter Garden Pavilion in the centre. 'But each of the buildings was ever so slightly different', says Butler. 'Now, all that we did was begin to propose a stronger, dominant figure for the park that would allow the buildings to find the edges in concert and begin to unite them all, so that, once designed by a different architect, they would hold together and create a dominant form for the public space.'

This proved to be a key move. It was some time after this early work on the park and how it would meld with the emerging masterplan that Butler returned to Liverpool and made a presentation at the Albert Dock alongside Cesar Pelli and Fred Clarke from the practice.

Changes began to happen quickly now. The bus station was moved further south, outside of the park and, to answer a growing interest in how this area would connect with surrounding districts, the team began looking at a radial hub with a very strong focus, the elliptical centre, with streets extending out in other directions to tie into them. 'We spent quite a lot of time strengthening the axis just east of the Law Courts so that could then extend the focus on the cathedral', says Butler. 'We created a cross-access, north-south, adjacent to the multi-storey car park that was ultimately done by Wilkinson Eyre, and pulling that in began to separate that southern building. Instead of a large mega-structure, it was broken into two distinct blocks.'

Thus, John Lewis emerged as a stand alone retail building with a hotel at Site 11, closer to the Mersey but with longer extension so it became a linear building and more wall-like in its enclosure of the park. PCP also took the building destined for Site 12, a residential scheme called 12 Park West. 'We began to look at it as an L-shaped block that held the ellipse to the north but then, as it wrapped in, it turned to create a wall in the Strand building.'

Thus that building emerged as a strong anchor to this corner of the park site, the aim being to complete the ellipse but be lower than the Law Courts and yet still provide some degree of public activity and function, such as allowing for pedestrians walking along that upper realm. Ultimately the building's distinctive, tapering design would also encourage circulation up from the Strand.

The ellipse meanwhile, would, so the thinking went, connect all of the different access points and modes of circulation - both vehicular and pedestrian - and the plan evolved so that all pedestrian uses were retained within it. The ellipse would also complement what Butler calls the 'slightly romantic, slightly organic sense of origin' of this part of the site and would also serve to frame and create a 'portal', collecting views out to the river and 'announcing' the project from the Strand and waterfront.

It was important that the park space would be an active one, with restaurants and cafés at Strand level and BDP's own restaurant building at the upper level of the park. Another alteration to the original masterplan was that the sweep of the arc extended further north to include Debenhams. Indeed, the complexity of the level changes involved across the whole of the park is considerable. 'The ellipse continued to become the uppermost floor of the retail building done by Allies and Morrison', adds Butler. 'By doing that, it created a leisure terrace on the upper level that visually spans the canyon of South John Street but feels as though it is the same level as the upper level of the park.'

In parallel with the emerging masterplan, BDP was already engaged in the early concept work for the park infrastructure, the 2000-space car park and service areas below. These extend the full width between Strand Street and Paradise Street supporting, literally, the park, South John Street and the main leisure building beyond. 'This was one of the most challenging areas for the masterplan team', Davenport recalls. 'Many hours were spent refining and further refining the emerging geometry and exploring ways of minimising the impact of the support areas on the park environment.'

'That was an incredible challenge', says Butler. Character, a sense of place and easy access to transportation are often difficult bedfellows in city-making. 'So being able to build a park that feels natural; that feels accessible and active in its use and still, beneath it, to have 2000 cars was a real challenge.' How, then, was this resolved? Rather than drawing air from the southern slope, the notion of a 'moat' adjacent to the retail pavilion on the park's northern edge emerged - the BDP-designed restaurant could deal with a large percentage of the supply and exhaust fumes. Removing it and allowing space inside this well and adding bamboo plantings to create a sense of green could kill two birds with one stone. The result is nearly 100sq m of ventilation grilles, fully concealed from the public's view. A conical focus created by BDP as the point of entry and exit to the park also rises up to park level to form a skylight, while sustainable elements include the very fact that the development has a green roof in such a city centre environment. This mediates run-off, collects water and slows down the ultimate percolation into the water system, allowing a certain filtration. It also provides some ambient cooling to the space below, and creating a green park in the centre of any city can reduce the heat island effect. The close proximity of public transport - the bus station - is considered another sustainable measure.

Accessibility was another key challenge, with BDP and PCP working hard to ensure that mobility-challenged users - whether that is people in wheelchairs or mums with prams - should enjoy 24-hour access to every part of the site. The Disability Discrimination Act (DDA),

102 for example, was a necessarily key driver in this move, and Butler is clear that the development goes well beyond the act's strictures. 'One of the things we spent a great deal of time on was lacing paths from the Strand up through to the head of the park', says Butler, 'and I think it is done naturally. It is not a second-class citizen event but rather celebrated with plantings and furniture so that to walk is enjoyable, as it would be for anyone else.'

Davenport identifies this stage of the project and the collaboration with PCP as a particularly rewarding period. 'Looking at the completed routes and spaces, the founding principles of the masterplan have proved robust. The lower level circuit of Paradise Street, defined by the historic inlet, the connection from Lord Street feeding the upper level circuit, and the link to Derby Square, the historic headland and the castle, have all been achieved as a natural transition.'

Indeed, Butler feels that the whole Liverpool One scheme has emerged with credit in many different areas. 'I think it is absolutely brilliant, to be honest', he says. 'That Grosvenor has invested the time and the care to involve so many parties in the creation of something that feels seamless in its level of integration.'

BDP's role as masterplanner has been no simple task in retaining this level of seamlessness. 'It is not easy, and the other thing is that they did not mandate or have a heavy hand in making it uniform', says Butler. 'There is a vitality to it. Most cities evolve over time - of course you get different architects and different materials, but to build so much - two million sq ft at once - it is rare to have it look as though it has evolved over decades.'

Top left: Aerial view over Albert Dock towards the PSDA site prior to construction. (Source unknown).

Top middle & bottom left: A pre-construction aerial of the site with Chavasse Park marked and highlighting it as the most significant piece of green space in the city centre. (Source unknown).

Far right: Extracts from Pelli Clarke Pelli concept analysis showing some of the various urban design studies that informed the emerging masterplan. (PCP).

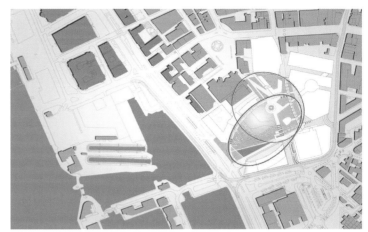

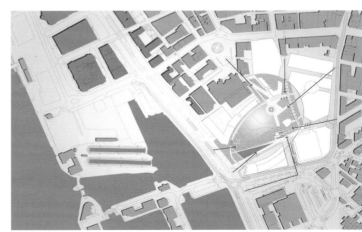

From the outset of the masterplan the park was seen as the centrepiece of the project and the green lung of the city. The challenge for the team was to provide a stunning green space with access for all, improved connectivity, variety and continuous active frontage whilst concealing 2000 parking spaces, servicing and two levels of active shopping below.

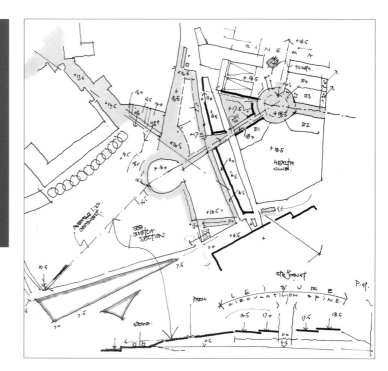

This page: Top right; *Critical early study examining the stepped section through the park and leisure terrace. These early BDP drawings stood the test of time with the finished park datums constructed largely as the sketch. (BDP).*

Opposite: top left; *BDP and Pelli Clarke Pelli examined numerous solutions to achieve access for all throughout the park. (BDP/PCP).*

Opposite: top right; *The final park layout integrating private, grand, formal, informal, terraced, flat, graded, active and event spaces in a single environment. (BDP).*

North south section through the park (looking towards South John Street) showing the concealment of all the ventilation requirements for the car park within the adjacent pavilion. Tenant plant for South John Street is also concealed at roof level. (BDP).

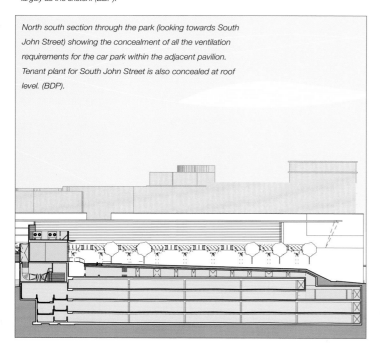

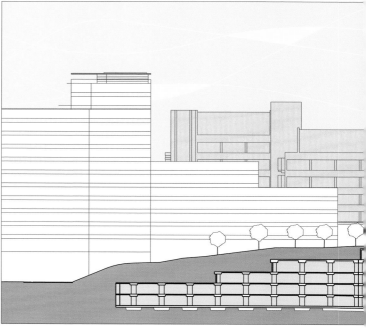

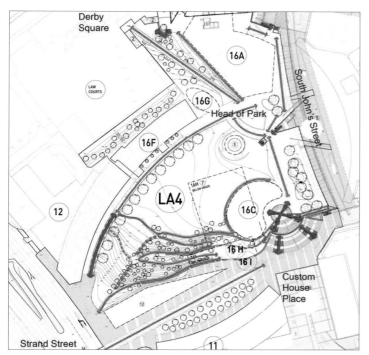

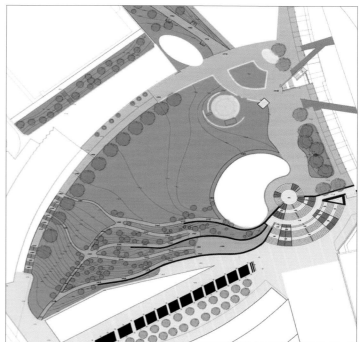

Derby Square

LAW COURTS

16A

16G

Head of Park

16F

South John's Street

LA4

16C

16 H

16 I

12

11

Custom House Place

Strand Street

Developed park section illustrating the 2000 parking spaces below, fully concealed servicing, the 'cone' as point of arrival and the retail and leisure fronting the street and park; all overlooking the World Heritage setting. (BDP).

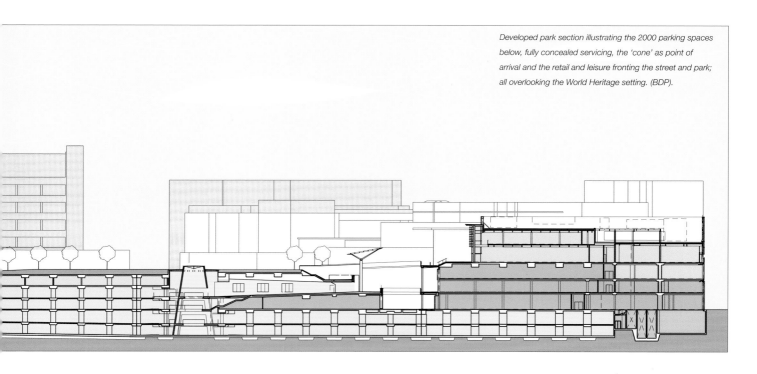

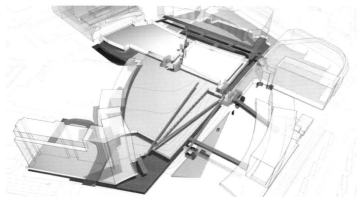

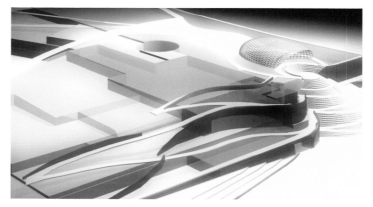

This page: Top left; Analysis diagram illustrating the servicing
and access capacity below the park. (PCP).
Top right; Further concept work to identify potential volumes
and accommodation beneath the park. This ultimately
created the two active leisure frontages onto the south facing
terrace. (PCP).
Bottom; Looking northward onto the park. (PCP).

Opposite page: Context
and scale of the surrounding
buildings framing the new
Chavasse Park. (Final image
version, Uniform).

Time to relax and enjoy.

A new natural landscape in
Liverpool city centre.

Public & Private – the park
has space for everyone.

Urban Cool – the park
at night.

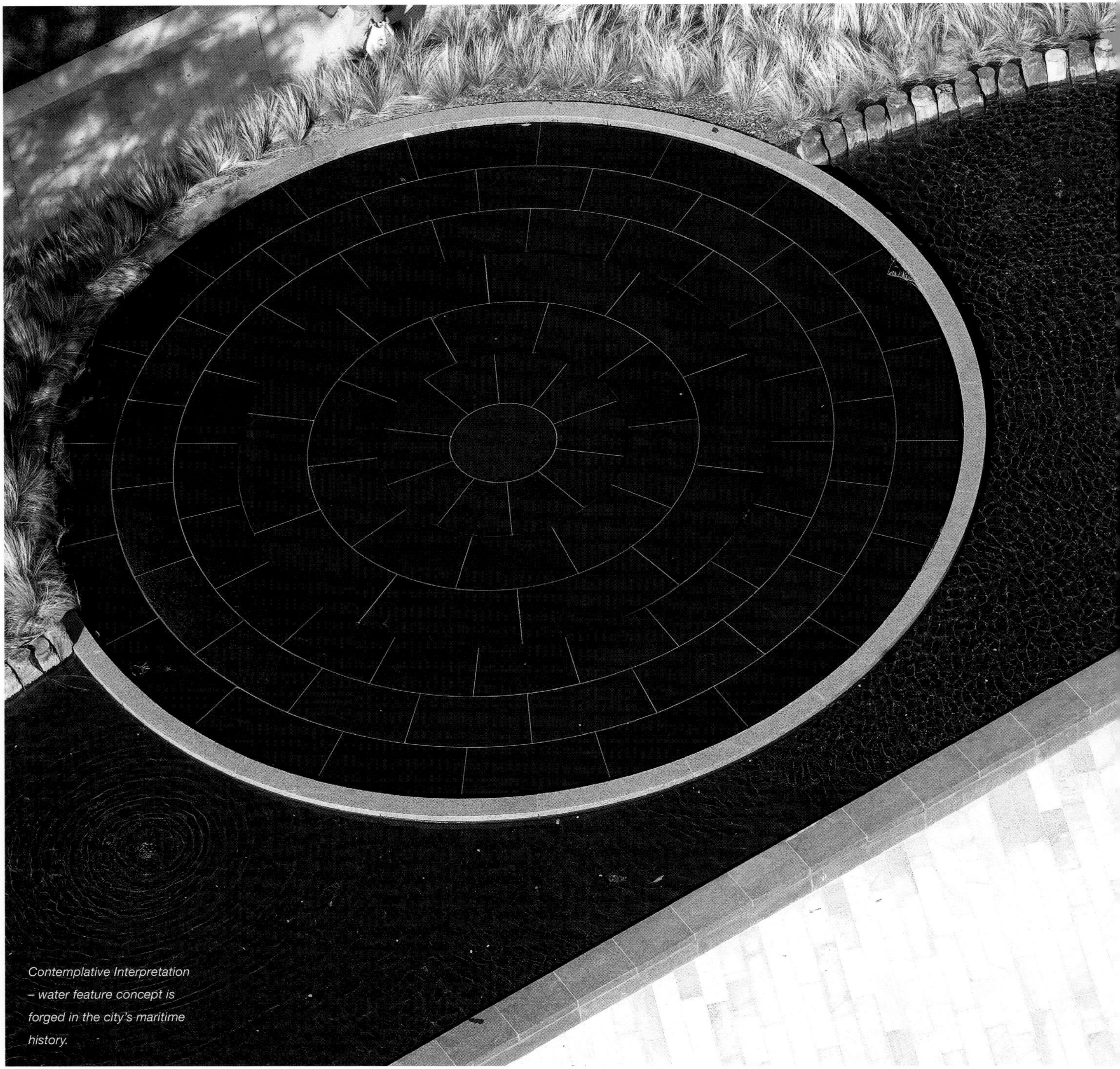

*Contemplative Interpretation
– water feature concept is
forged in the city's maritime
history.*

Natural Environment - the park providing strong resonances with the city's historic landscape.

active
streets

Shoppers enjoying
the new city streets in
Liverpool One.

the retailer's perspective

A well designed, permeable, and attractive retail-led scheme is all very well, but if it doesn't work for the retailers and shoppers themselves then it cannot be considered a true success. So how has Liverpool One fared in this regard thus far? The answer is pretty successfully, given the national and global picture of economic downturn.

Kevin O'Donovan is the general manager of the 185,000 sq ft Debenhams store on a corner block facing Lord Street and South John Street, and had not worked in the city before he joined on the project's long build-up in September 2007. 'Up until then I'd never even been to Liverpool, actually', he admits. He admits too to not having had a particularly favourable view of the city prior to his arrival, citing negative headlines and his perception of a place with more than its fair share of crime. 'They were very friendly and by the same token proud, passionate people, but perhaps with a reputation for crime and violence. It was maybe a city that you might not feel safe in at the wrong time or location. Having said that, my opinions 12 months on are pretty different.'

Now Ilkley-based O'Donovan stays in Liverpool four nights a week and has seen his opinions change, partially through having spent many nights out in the city: 'I've never, ever felt threatened; I've only ever had good times. I now have a generally different perspective.' Unlike many other cities, he feels that Liverpudlians are a welcoming, friendly lot, and O'Donovan believes it is a city on the up.

So much for the wider city. How about the retailing perspective of Liverpool One? The Debenhams store, designed by Groupe 6 in conjunction with BDP, employs almost 600 people on the Liverpool One site to cope with the large floorspace and shopper numbers. O'Donovan says there is always a 'halo effect' on opening new stores and Liverpool was no different, especially given the huge expectation, marketing and PR around the event. 'It was the biggest thing to have opened in the UK for a long, long time', he says. 'Probably since they regenerated the centre of Birmingham with the Bullring.' This expectation and excitement translated into a 'very, very busy first couple of months from the end of May to the end of July', but, understandably, national and global economic pressures had an effect on performance following that period. 'Sales were very good to start with; then they've been challenging, like they have been everywhere else. But overall we're really pleased in the five months that we've been trading in Liverpool.'

Footfall has been good overall, too. O'Donovan reports that the Liverpool figures are certainly ahead of those in other Debenhams stores around the country in other big cities. 'We've exceeded the target and projections we set ourselves in Liverpool', he says. Why? 'I'd put that down to a number of things: pent-up demand in Liverpool – the shopping offer was pretty poor in all sectors – and there had been no investment. With the exception of the Met Quarter, it hadn't really changed much in 20 years.' What O'Donovan calls the Scouse passion and desire to be loyal to Liverpool drew some of that pent-up demand, because, he says, the locals were previously shopping in Manchester and at the Trafford Centre. 'There has been some diversion and deflection from areas like Warrington and Chester too – I think people were keen to spend some money and have some choice about where to spend their money in Liverpool. Notwithstanding that, I think it is a super, super development as well. I think they're very proud of it, and they should be.'

The design of Liverpool One is a particularly praiseworthy element, with O'Donovan citing the fact that it is not a traditional covered shopping centre being one of its strongest points. 'I like the fact it links the city with the docks and is not a cosseted shopping centre environment. I like the fact that it is mostly open to the elements. I think it's in a great location and the quality of the shop-fitting, the build and the finish has been really good. You can see that in the way that the people of Liverpool are respecting it.'

The high quality of the project extends even to the car park, which O'Donovan commends as a well-planned, coordinated and thought-out element of the wider scheme.

Whilst being at Liverpool One has not made Debenhams think again about where they locate in future, the relatively higher investment the retailer made on the finish and the fittings of the Liverpool store has led to two recent awards for the design of the shop and its interior. Statistics about visitor numbers to the wider scheme also show that BDP's masterplan has been a successful strategy, with Experian numbers likely to show that Liverpool is rising up the national retail ladder.

Debenhams is just one of the many retailers to commend the vibrant environment that has been created. 'We're very happy and proud to be there and to be one of the main anchor tenants', says O'Donovan. 'Our relationship with Liverpool One and Grosvenor has been good and I think it will only ever do one thing – and that is to take Liverpool from strength to strength.'

The European appeal of the city and Liverpool One.

impact of the masterplan

116 Taking the opportunity to reflect, Davenport sees Liverpool One quite understandably as having been the project of a lifetime. 'It's not too often that you are able to lead a team and a project that quite simply generates a sea change of fortune in your own town or city', he says. Many have asked him what facet of the project he is most proud of and what one moment he recalls above any other. 'For me it was the 29th of May 2008, the day of the first phase opening', he says. 'Within minutes of cutting the ribbon, the streets were active and back to life, people enjoying the spaces, the city reconnected, Lord Street reinvigorated. Fundamentally, seeing the city on an upward curve once more - principally through Grosvenor's commitment and investment - was hugely rewarding.'

One of the cornerstones of the masterplan, the project's permeability and interaction with surrounding quarters, has been demonstrated clearly by published figures. These indicate, in addition to Liverpool One's own success, a significant rise in footfall to both the adjacent high street and the Albert Dock as a result of the masterplan and improved city connections.

Leading lights, 24/7
Successful city regeneration cannot be just about the quality of the daytime environment but how the spaces and streets live, work and function, 24/7. Liverpool's night-time economy is famous with particular quarters becoming magnets for social activity. 'Although the income per head in the city is relatively low against the national average, Liverpudlians know how to spend their money and enjoy it', says Davenport. Like so many other aspects of Liverpool One's evolution, the approach to the lighting design has embraced not just the context of the project but its city centre environs. With so many fine buildings and landmarks framing the site, a vital role of the masterplan was the establishment of vistas and visual references in both a daytime and night-time context. The BDP lighting team set about the task by initially undertaking an assessment of the city centre's lighting addressing feature buildings, public spaces and public highways. This evolved after several weeks of study into a comprehensive report identifying both the stronger and weaker areas and critically setting the context in which to integrate the Liverpool One lighting proposals.

The buildings and public realm areas across the entire site are connected by a lighting scheme designed by BDP and headed by lighting director Laura Bayliss. As Laura explains 'It was important for us to create a sense of intimacy and human scale in such a large development'.

Involved from the outset, BDP's lighting team were able to implement a design strategy that would link all aspects of the masterplan seamlessly. Part of the designers' task was to also relate the lighting of the redeveloped area with the existing lighting schemes of the surrounding areas and take into account Liverpool City Council's own lighting strategy. The proximity of existing lighting schemes inevitably impacted on the lighting design of the new quarters and it was important to create clear visual links between the development and existing areas.

The lighting scheme worked to highlight specific nodal points, the character of each of the zones or 'quarters' and key architectural features within each quarter. To ensure the lighting works in harmony with each building as well as the wider masterplan, Laura and her team collaborated across the wide group of architects at the earliest design stages to integrate lighting into the architecture. A 'no clutter' approach to the design was also important by incorporating light fittings seamlessly into the public realm, such as within benches and handrails, the lighting creates minimal visual impact during the daytime hours but maximum impact at night.

The main theory that underpins the lighting masterplan however is based on the 'phototropic effect'. In the same way that plants are drawn towards the light, the lighting designers at BDP saw that people are too. This theory informed decisions on which facades should be lit, which routes should have a cool brighter light over other routes and considered light in relation to people and vehicular movement.

Lighting is also used to affect and encourage movement between previously unrelated areas and to certain aspects of the scheme. An example of this can be seen on the cinema bridge link. Careful integration of lighting equipment into the underside and perimeter of the bridge draws attention to the Liverpool One Information Centre below.

Cool and warm light were used to differentiate the hierarchy of routes through the project. The feature lighting demonstrates a sensitive use of colour to highlight the more active leisure areas and main viewpoints.

118 **This page:** *Soffit treatment to cinema link bridge above Wall Street.*

Opposite page: Top left; *Dramatic impact of ' the cut', the zig-zag leisure connection from Paradise Street to park level.*

Bottom left: *Dramatic lighting to the lift core and Galleria leisure space, linking the park with Paradise Street.*

Far right: *Ever changing. The zig-zag stair from Paradise Street.*

Opposite page: Top; *Further views of Paradise Street and the zig-zag leisure connection*
Bottom: *looking back down the cut towards Paradise Street, College Lane and ultimate Ropewalks connectivity.*

This page: Looking north on the leisure terrace towards Debenhams and the wonderful North John Street skyline.

122

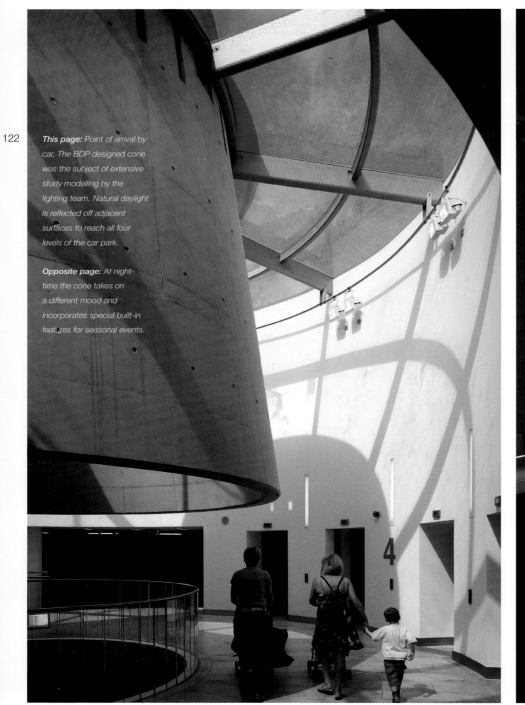

This page: *Point of arrival by car. The BDP designed cone was the subject of extensive study modelling by the lighting team. Natural daylight is reflected off adjacent surfaces to reach all four levels of the car park.*

Opposite page: *At night-time the cone takes on a different mood and incorporates special built-in features for seasonal events.*

124

Liverpool has the greatest density of Grade 1 listed buildings outside London and a world famous sky line. So why not celebrate it? Davenport goes on to explain. 'I was determined from the very early days of the project to ensure that the city's landmarks were celebrated and enjoyed as part of the project. In any urban environment, enclosed or open, a sense of orientation is vital. What better than to achieve this by views onto some of Liverpool's most famous buildings?'

Although now simply framed, these vistas took several years of careful planning and execution across many teams to achieve.

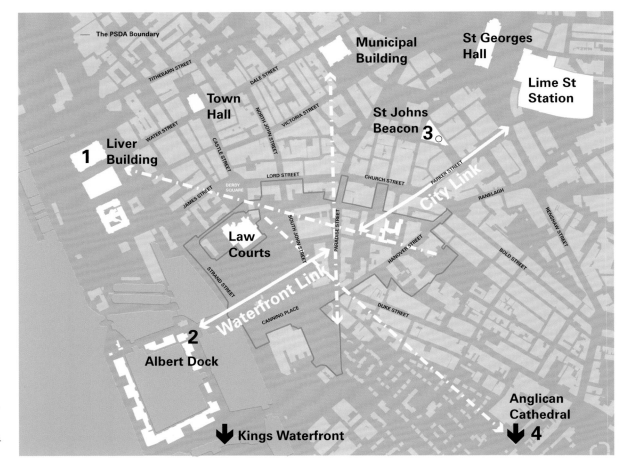

Extract from the masterplan. Diagram defining the important visual connections from within and outside of the site curtilage. (BDP).

The magnificent skyline
of North John Street looking
beyond Debenhams' Lord
Street entrance.

Connecting with the city.
This page: top; *new and old framing Paradise Street.*

Bottom right; *Glimpsing the city skyline from the park.*

Bottom left; *Dramatic view of the Liver Building, the ultimate Liverpool landmark, from College Lane.*

You need to visit the Odeon to see this one. The Sky Bar offers views towards the Anglican Cathedral, the southern skyline and the Mersey Estuary.

beyond 2008

beyond 2008... one city: a greater city of liverpool?

Liverpool One reflects a long-term vision for the city and, like any major project, it will take time to bed in, for the landscaping to mature and for locals to get to grips with the new part of city they have inherited.

But beyond the opening, and beyond the year of Liverpool's Capital of Culture tag, what will be the legacy? Just what is on the horizon next for this constantly changing region?

Andrew Teage, urbanism director with BDP, is charged with a lot of the front-end, visionary planning and regeneration work for the practice. His task has been, in part, to cement BDP's position in the city and on Merseyside.

One of these areas of interest is Liverpool's North Shore. This is the area from the edge of the Liverpool CBD or city centre, right the way up to the South Sefton boundary, adjacent to the wards of Everton, Kirkdale and Anfield. It is a 330 hectare site for which BDP has prepared a vision framework for Liverpool Land Development Company before it was brought into part of the new Liverpool Vision. 'It was to set the 50-year vision of what that area could be', says Teage, 'which has subsequently generated an infrastructure study looking at the key elements of primary transport infrastructure that would need to service an expanded city centre into North Shore.'

North Liverpool, which includes North Shore, is one of Liverpool Vision's key action areas and BDP is keen to maintain its dialogue with the organisation to try to see it into fruition, providing a framework for investment and development. This would sit alongside things like Peel Holdings' Liverpool Waters project, a 150-acre site that stretches from Princes Dock in the south to Bramley Moore Dock in the north.

BDP has also sought to look beyond traditional regeneration relationships and begun engaging with organisations such as the Liverpool Biennial, who are interested in examining how public art might be used to kick-start regeneration in the north Liverpool area. 'In that context, BDP has begun to evaluate the regeneration potential along the Leeds Liverpool canal', says Teage.

In seeking to contribute to areas beyond Liverpool One and North Shore, Teage has been looking at housing market renewal areas in South Sefton in terms of masterplanning and supplementary planning documents, alongside other masterplanning and architectural work over the water in Woodside. 'It is really looking at Liverpool and Wirral, Birkenhead, down as far as Widnes and up to Southport as being one city, plugging into the city region agenda.'

The general aim is to move beyond this bedrock by engaging with organisations, individuals, businesses outside of normal professional relationships. BDP kick started this process with a Christmas event looking at Ropewalks past, present and future held jointly with Renew North West, RIBA and FACT

This page and opposite:
Long term potential of
Liverpool's Waterfront. (BDP).

Opposite: Far right;
Connectivity and integration
in a city wide context -
taken from BDP's visioning
framework study for
'Northshore'. Liverpool
as 'One City' with the
potential for one of the finest
waterfronts in the world.

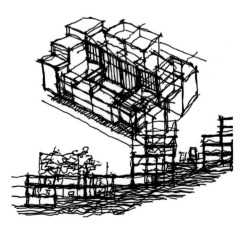

(Foundation for Art & Creative Technology), inviting the wider business, cultural and creative community of Ropewalks to debate where the area should be aiming and how could BDP help in that process?

'We're here in the city, we're a key part of the city, and we want to be involved in the wider regeneration', says Teage. The urbanism group's role is to facilitate this process, learning lessons from Ropewalks and applying them to wider development work in areas as far as Speke, North Huyton, and Widnes. 'We feel passionate about the city', says Teage. 'We think about how these things impact on the whole city, not just the particular project that we're working on.' BDP has followed this up with its 10th birthday celebration party, this time exploring the success of the city's renaissance and looking to its future.

The Royal Liverpool and Broadgreen University Hospital is another organisation looking at wholesale change. BDP has assisted in this objective as its interim planning and masterplanning advisors, on the back of the practice's strength in healthcare work. The hospital is redeveloping at the eastern gateway to the city, aiming to replace its facilities on its current site and BDP is hopeful in again becoming involved in such a face-changing project for Liverpool. The practice's work at Aintree Racecourse is another city-scale scheme.

'It's picking up some key, large-scale architectural schemes that we've been involved in and applying them to a wider spatial context, particularly their role in transforming the nature of a city, and then delivering against this to ensure BDP's legacy as key agents of change within Liverpool.'

The cultural link has also spread to China particularly in 2006 when Liverpool and Shanghai's sister city relationship was formalised by the Liverpool-Shanghai Partnership. This cultural link and relationship will be furthered, when Liverpool, with the oldest Chinese community in Britain, will be one of only two UK cities to host a pavilion at the 2010 World Expo in Shanghai. BDP is again hopeful that it can help the city council put together a story on the back of its work at Liverpool One, Ropewalks and North Shore, to present Liverpool in the best possible way on the global stage, under an urban regeneration best practice banner. 'That's another exciting step forward for Liverpool', says Teage. 'It will put Liverpool firmly back in the international eye.'

When it comes to Liverpool One as a significant, city-changing project, Teage feels that it has helped cut what had become the barrier of Strand Street and the old park from the city centre, effectively integrating the Ropewalks and Bluecoat Triangle. 'I think that the way that the masterplan, from the very first principles, has looked at integrating Church Street, Lord Street, Ropewalks and, to a lesser extent, the Baltic Triangle areas, has been

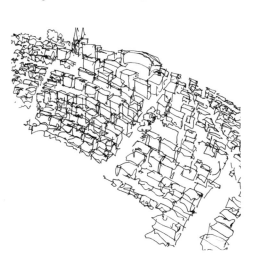

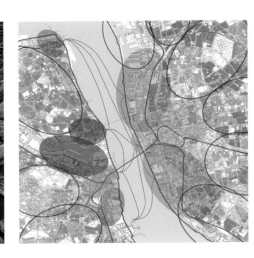

132

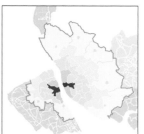    

very successful. If you walk down Seel Street and Duke Street, you don't get the feeling that you're moving from a smaller-grade cultural area into a big retail development; it doesn't hit you. It's a gradual change. You're then suddenly into this dramatic retail environment and then, crikey, you're onto this fantastic waterfront.'

Finally, another viewpoint from another key Liverpool fixture: David Wade Smith, a retailer in Liverpool for many years - in the 80s and 90s as part of the Wade Smith retail designer and sportswear group that was sold to Arcadia in the late 90s - is clear about the impact Liverpool One has had and will continue to have, going forward. As a founding member of Liverpool Vision and board member from 1999 until 2008, plus chairman of Liverpool's Chamber of Commerce, Wade Smith is certainly well-placed. But he condenses successful city-making into only a few key constituents. 'One of my principal expressions is that great places to visit are great places to live, work and invest',

he says. This, he believes, underpins the importance of the visitor economy. 'Liverpool One is the biggest single investment by financial scale that the city has ever seen', he says. How has it been achieved?

The success of the scheme, Wade Smith believes, has been down to partnerships pulling in the same direction, but he too has his eyes on the future. 'The great thing about the Capital of Culture bid', he says, 'was that it was 2008 in relation to our timing but it was again intended to be a midway point, a milestone on the way to a longer vision extended specifically to 2015 but also beyond, setting us up for the 21st century. It has been nothing short of miraculous.'

Teage agrees that regenerating Liverpool is an ongoing process and that the next step is almost as important as those that have come before. The Northern Way is one initiative that has the potential to encourage city regions to come together for the maximum benefit

of the wider area and BDP's urbanism group encourages such cross-border synergy in the regeneration and masterplanning work it undertakes in the region. Another might be the legacy of the Capital of Culture celebrations, which segued neatly with BDP's own 10th birthday in Liverpool and the launch of Liverpool One. There is work to be done, however, in shining the regeneration light a little further afield, providing infrastructure and connecting the key district centres with the heartland. 'Liverpool city centre has achieved a lot, but the Knowsleys, the St Helens', the Huytons, the Seftons that sit on the city boundary – they aren't integrated with that exciting change that is happening in the city centre', says Teage. 'For Liverpool to take that next step there needs to be a lot more cross-boundary collaboration and partnership, sharing the benefits of the city's success and ensuring that the suburbs and the inner city continue that regeneration journey.'

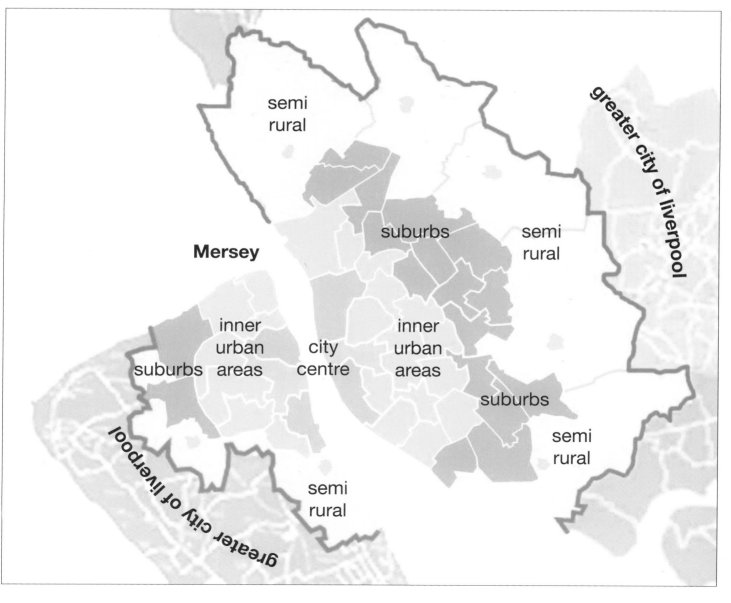

134   The city's basic infrastructure is therefore critically important. In this context the city is fortunate. Liverpool's arteries and veins - its goods and passenger transport infrastructure stretching back to 1938 - were magnificent. With some foresight, and a little fortuitous neglect, the city has retained the basics of an infrastructure befitting a second city of Empire. But if Liverpool is to come back and stay, if the population drain is to be significantly reversed and if the city of Liverpool is to be more than a million again, the city needs it all back - and that includes the trams. It needs re-opened lines, re-opened stations, re-opened tunnels, the overhead back on the waterfront, better freight connections and, ultimately, another Mersey crossing. Amazingly, because most of the unused tunnels, stations, rail beds, loop lines, tracks and alignments are still there, the cost per capita would be lower than anywhere else in Britain. This is a huge advantage for Liverpool of which central government ought to be aware.

    Ultimately, BDP is well placed to help ensure the city stays on track. 'We've been involved with major change in Liverpool for the last ten years and we want to continue to engage with that in this exciting time, post-2008, through new initiatives, through North Shore, Liverpool's Southern Gateway and wider masterplanning in some of these suburban authorities', says Teage. 'We want to try and push home that the city centre really needs to connect with the rest of the city region. Otherwise, it is not going to take that next step.'

Left: Liverpool's extensive rail infrastructure built to support the phenomenal growth of dock traffic. Much of this infrastructure, including tunnels, remains intact. (Source unknown).
Above: Re-connecting the city with its inner urban, suburban and rural centres is critical to a sustainable, prosperous and equitable city and city region. (BDP).

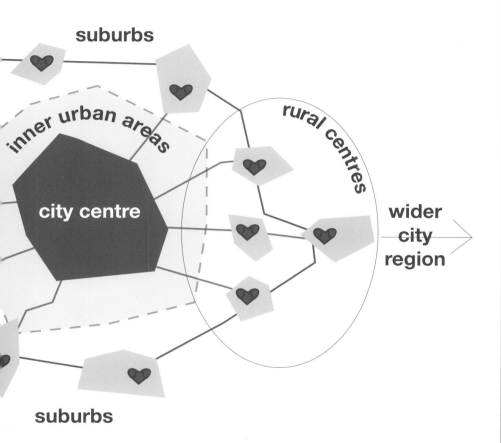

suburbs

inner urban areas

rural centres

city centre

wider city region

suburbs

There is work to be done in shining the regeneration light a little further afield, providing infrastructure and connecting the key district centres with the heartland. Liverpool city centre has achieved a lot, but the Knowsleys, the St Helens', the Huytons, the Seftons that sit on the city boundary - their integration is another major challenge that lies ahead. For Liverpool to take that next step there needs to be a lot more cross-boundary collaboration and partnership, sharing the benefits of the city's success and ensuring that the suburbs and the inner cities continue that regeneration journey...

epilogue

In an age when the general thrust in retail is towards homogeneity - where a high street in one part of the country can look pretty much like another, many hundreds of miles away, it is heartening that the idea of 'place' can still be a driver in a large, city centre urban regeneration scheme. Whilst it would have almost certainly been far easier to create one large, monolithic project, carried out by a single design hand, it is much to Grosvenor and the city council's credit – and BDP's humility and ingenuity - to recognise that cities are in the main made up of many different atmospheres, materials and styles. So it is with Liverpool One. In the final reckoning and across this major development site, there is no loud clunking of gears. Rather, there is an admirable, slick (but not corporate), and gradual change from quarter to quarter, unified by civic, pedestrian-friendly permeability, and underpinned by technical know-how and a green lung of a park. And, whilst the crossing of the Strand is not perfect, the city is in touch with its waterfront once more, and the wartime bombings that did so much damage, dislocating and disconnecting Liverpool, look to have been replaced by a vibrant chunk of city, neatly knitted back into the urban fabric once more. In the course of researching this book it became clear to this writer the crucial ingredient of success was a design champion holding the vision together, taking the city with him, enriched by the design skills of over twenty architects under BDP's robust - but challengeable - masterplan.

Eight hundred years on from the city's inception, what has resulted is part of a long-term vision for the future. Liverpool, at last, looks to be back - on the very spot it embarked from.

David Taylor

acknowledgments

the team

core masterplanning team

Grosvenor

BDP
masterplanners

Capita Symonds
highways designers and health and safety advisers

Davis Langdon
cost consultants

Drivers Jonas
planning consultants

Nightingale Associates
access consultants

Pelli Clarke Pelli Architects
urban design consultants

Tenos
fire strategy consultants

Waterman Partnership
structural and environmental engineers

WSP Group
infrastructure and building services engineers

property / planning consultants

Edmund Kirby

CBRE

Cushman & Wakefield

Keppie Massie

Strutt & Parker

Tushingham Moore

contractors

Balfour Beatty
east of Paradise Street

Kier
Hilton Hotel

Laing O'Rourke
west of Paradise Street

Mansell
Site 8

site	architects
1	*Dixon Jones*
2	*Page \ Park*
3, 3A / B	*Haworth Tompkins*
4A	*Brock Carmichael Architects*
4B	*Brock Carmichael Architects*
4C	*Brock Carmichael Architects*
5A / B	*Stephenson Bell*
5A façade	*Hawkins \ Brown*
6	*Glenn Howells Architects*
7 / 7A	*Haworth Tompkins with Brock Carmichael Architects*
8	*Greig & Stephenson*
8 (pavilion)	*FAT*
9	*CZWG Architects LLP*
10	*John McAslan + Partners*
10A	*Wilkinson Eyre Architects*
11	*Squire and Partners*
12	*Pelli Clarke Pelli Architects*
13A	*BDP*
13B	*Allies and Morrison*
13C	*BDP*
13D	*BDP*
14	*BDP*
14B façade	*Marks Barfield Architects*
15	*Groupe 6 with BDP*
16F	*BDP*
16G	*Studio Three*
17	*Wilkinson Eyre.Architects*
17A	*Wilkinson Eyre.Architects*
18	*Leach Rhodes Walker*
19 / 20	*Austin-Smith:Lord*
21 / 22	*To be appointed*

Other teams:
Craig Foster Architects
Owen Ellis Partnership

executive architect role

site	architect
6	BDP
10	BDP
11	Aedas
12	Brock Carmichael Architects
13B	BDP

engineers

Arup

FHP

Hoare Lea

Paul Moy Associates

Pell Frischmann

MASTERPLAN TEAM			EXECUTIVE ROLE	LANDSCAPE MASTERPLAN	LIGHTING MASTERPLAN
Overall Responsibility *Terry Davenport*	**Concept & Executive Role**		**Overall Responsibility** *Stephen Gillham*	Phil Moss	Barrie Wilde Elga Niemann
Peter Drummond Richard Rees	**Site 13A** Andrew Barber Chris Hernon Chloe Yearsley Gary Wilding Jeremy Sweet	Rhodri Evans Richard Lloyd Russell Cross Sasa Simeunovic Terry Lynch Tom Bates Tom Corbett Tom Higgins	**Site 6** Adam Hiley David Cummins John Doyle Kevin Blinkhorn Ronan Connelly Sam Huscroft	**Landscape Concept Overall Responsibility** *Paul Taylor* Adam Vickers Darrell Wilson Franziska Schoder Kate Pinnock Paul Taylor Sally Bower	**Lighting Concept Overall Responsibility** *Laura Bayliss* Brendan Keely Chris Lowe Karen Ilhau Katja Nurminen Laura Bayliss Laura Mackay Melisa Stears
Andrew Barber Ed Butler Frances McGowan Jamie Scott Katrina Thompson Melanie Boulton Rob Shackleton Roy Taylor Saxbourne Cheung Steve Gillham	**Site 13C** Austin Holmes David Ng Gavin Elliott Karen Harper Mark Davies Natalia Maximova Neil Serridge Peter Horrocks Rhodri Evans Terry Lynch Tony Marshall	**Site 14** Alistair Elder Andrew Barber Brenda Coughlan David Mayers Gareth Gazey Jonathan Rawstram Kevin Blinkhorn Sandy Fergusson Tom Greig	**Site 10** Gareth Jackson John Doyle Mike McDonald Ronan Connelly Sam Huscroft Terry Lynch Tim Humphries Tom Bates Tom Corbett	**Landscape Executive Role Overall Responsibility** *Karen Howell* Adam Vickers Carl Horsdal Darren Lynskey David Wilson Ian Foster James Millington Jenny Ferguson Sally Bower	**Lighting Delivery** Brendan Keely Chris Lowe Karen Ilhau Katja Nurminen Laura Bayliss
Shop front Handbook / Tenant Liaison Ben Lilley Bob Goulden Rob Shackleton	**Site 13D** Austin Holmes Chris Lloyd Christian Grootveldt David Cornett David Ng Graham Cavanagh Jonathon McCrone Julie Winrow Ken Taylor Kevin Blinkhorn Kevin Horton Larry Cupit Paul McMullen Peter McGurk	**Site 15 Groupe 6/BDP** Damien Gaudin Dave Cummins Eamon Doyle Ian John Jenni Adshead Mark Crocker Mark Wilson Stephen Charles **Site 16F** Julien Marchand Peter Woodcock Russell Cross	**Site 13B** Anita Ng Barry Oldham Chris Lloyd Jessie Qui John Ellam Jonathon McCrone Luke Green Matt Oliver Matt Rowe Tom Higgins	**Support to Chavasse Park Executive Team** Willerby Landscapes with ALD	**BDP Co-Management** Chris Slack Gareth Hughes Hossam Abdalla Norman Hewetson Terry Shinn

BDP's role in Liverpool One:
- *Masterplanners*
- *Architects for sites; 13a, 13c, 13d, 14, 15 (in collaboration with Groupe 6) and 16f*
- *Executive architects for sites; 6, 10 and 13b*
- *Concept landscape design for all public realm areas, Chavasse Park in collaboration with Pelli Clarke Pelli*
- *Executive landscape delivery across the whole project*
- *Lighting masterplan*
- *Concept lighting design for 16 sites*

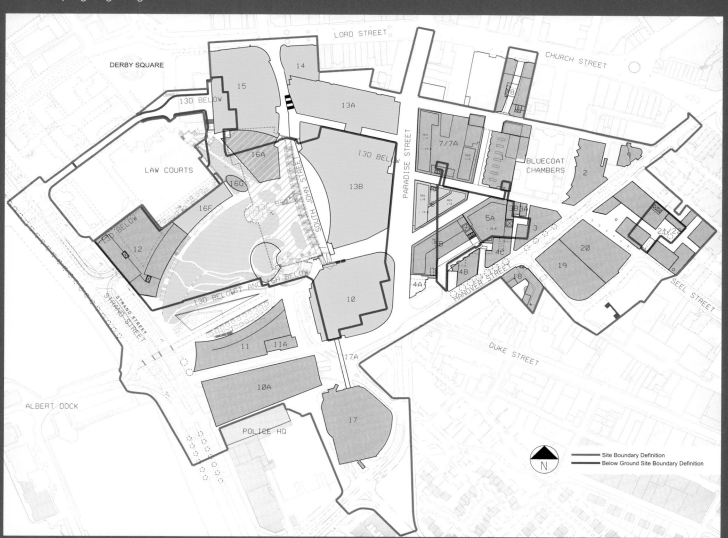

picture credits

interview list

bibliography

about the author

The author and the publisher gratefully acknowledge the people who gave their permission to reproduce material in this book. Whilst every effort has been made to contact copyright holders for their permission to reprint material, the publishers would be grateful to hear from any copyright holder who is not acknowledged here and will undertake to rectify any errors or omissions in future editions.

l = left,
r = right,
t = top,
b = bottom

All drawings are courtesy of the relevant architects, published with their permission

Photography
p 2 © Mills Media

p 20 © Bruno Vincent / getty images

p 28(t) © David Millington Photography. Courtesy of Brock Carmichael Architects

pp 5, 28(b), 108(l), 109 (l), 110, 111, 113, 115, 118, 119(l), 119(b), 122, 123, 125, 126, 127, back cover © BDP (David Barbour)

p 29 © Richard Cooper, Photoflex for Urban Splash

pp 99, 109(r), 119(r), 120, 121
© David Thrower at Redshift Photography Ltd

p 108(r) © BDP (Sanna Fisher-Payne)

p 117 © webbaviation.co.uk

p 144 © David Millington Photography

Bill Butler (PCP)

Terry Davenport (BDP)

Jim Gill (Liverpool Vision)

Rod Holmes (Grosvenor)

Graham Haworth (Haworth Tomkins)

Ken Moth (BDP)

Kevin O'Donovan (Debenhams)

David Page (Page \ Park)

Richard Rees (BDP)

Trevor Skempton (LCC)

Mike Storey (LCC)

Andy Teage (BDP)

David Wade Smith

additional contributions to text - Chapter 4

Planning strategy;
Julia Chowings
(Drivers Jonas).

Liverpool 800 – Culture, Character & History, edited by John Belchem ISBN 1-84631-035-0 Liverpool University Press

David Taylor is a journalist who specialises in writing about architecture, property and design. A former acting editor of The Architects' Journal, he has curated exhibitions on subjects such as the Thames Gateway, London's suburbs, and the office of the future at the New London Architecture Gallery, edits the London Property Review, is business editor of World Architecture News and contributes regularly to other magazines in the UK and US. He was on CABE's writers' panel for four years and has contributed to books including '1001 buildings you must see before you die' (Cassell Illustrated), and Architecture and Commerce - New Office Design in London (Wordsearch).

Special thanks to my colleague Rob Shackleton, for his assistance in the production of this publication.

Terry Davenport.